Collins *gem*

Chinese Astrology

HarperCollins*Publishers*
Westerhill Road, Bishopbriggs, Glasgow G64 2QT.

www.collins.co.uk

A Diagram book first created by Diagram Visual
Information Limited of 195 Kentish Town Road,
London NW5 2JU

Illustrations by Bernard Lodge

First published 1996
This edition published 2004

Reprint 10 9 8 7 6 5 4 3 2

© Diagram Visual Information Limited 1996, 1999, 2004

ISBN 0-00-717849-2

Printed in Italy by Amadeus S.r.l.

Foreword

Collins Gem Chinese Astrology is an introduction to
the 12 symbolic animals and the five elements that are
the basis of Oriental astrology. Although this
astrological system originated in China, it is widely
practised in other Asian countries that, historically,
came under the influence of China. For example,
many Japanese and Vietnamese people use Chinese
astrology as a guide to interpreting their lives. For this
reason, it is often referred to as Oriental astrology.

Chinese astrology is concerned with the influence of
the Moon in a 12-year cycle. Simple tables of dates
enable readers to quickly find which of the 12 animals
rules the year of their birth: rat, ox, tiger, rabbit,
dragon, snake, horse, goat, monkey, rooster, dog or
pig. The 12 animals, their attributes and the
significance of the five elements are each described in
separate chapters. Many areas of life – from a rat's
general personality traits and interests at work, to a
pig's behaviour when in love – are detailed with the
help of lists, panels and illustrations. Lists of famous
people born in the same animal years add to the
general interest.

Along with other Eastern philosophies, Chinese
astrology has recently become popular in the West.
Despite being complex in its analysis, it is easy for the
novice to access, as all you need is your date of birth.
Collins Gem Chinese Astrology brings the reader a
refreshing alternative to Western astrology.

Contents

Introduction

HISTORY

Astrology is one of the most ancient of the Chinese philosophies. It is at least 2000 years old. Originally, astrology was inseparable from astronomy. The two were considered to be one discipline. China has one of the oldest civilizations in the world and from very early on practitioners of astronomy/astrology were always present as officials of the imperial court.

In ancient China, astrology was used to reveal what was expected to happen to a nation. It was not until the beginning of the Christian era that astrology began to be used to give individual readings. By the time of the Tang dynasty (AD 618–907), a whole encyclopedia had been

The twelve animals of Chinese astrology

Rat   Ox   Tiger   Rabbit

Horse   Goat   Monkey   Rooster

written about the art of giving personal astrological readings.

LEGENDS

The origin of the 12 animal signs of Chinese astrology is unclear. Chinese legend attributes the creation of the signs to the Yellow Emperor in 2637 BC. The Yellow Emperor is a semimythical figure in Chinese history. Other legends accredit Buddha (c.563–c.483 BC) with the creation of the 12-animal cycle. Apparently, he invited all the animals to visit him but, for some reason, only 12 animals showed up. To thank them, Buddha gave each animal a year which would be dedicated to that animal alone throughout history. The years were allocated in the order in which the animals had arrived.

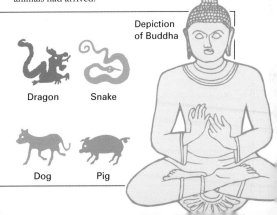

Depiction of Buddha

Dragon   Snake

Dog   Pig

How to use this book

In this book, we have considered five different aspects of the Chinese astrological chart. These are:

- the animal sign
- the natural element
- the dominant element
- Yin and Yang
- companion in life

Also, at the end of each animal chapter is a brief look at how the Western and Chinese zodiacs can be combined to give even more detailed readings.

All you need to know to access information about all these aspects is:

- year of birth
- date of birth
- hour of birth (the nearest hour or two is enough)

For example, if you were born on 30 July 1970 between the hours of 3 pm and 5 pm:

1 First, using your year of birth, find out what animal sign you are from the tables on pp. 10–14. In this instance, the person is a dog.

2 We know that the natural element of all dogs is metal and that they are Yang people (this information is included at the start of each animal chapter and is also shown by the chart on pp. 18–19).

3 Also from the year of birth, we know that the person's dominant element is metal (see the sections on elements in the relevant animal

chapter). In this case the dominant and natural element are both metal – but they are not always the same.

4 From the hour of birth, we know that the person's companion in life is the monkey (see the chart on pp. 24–25 to calculate your inner companion).

5 From the date of birth, we can calculate that the person is a Leo (see chart on p. 27 to work this out).

In this example, the person should read the chapters on the dog and the monkey to get a full Chinese astrological reading. Further information on the elements and Yin and Yang forces can be obtained by reading the relevant parts of this introduction.

ANIMAL SIGNS

The animal signs are the most basic aspect of Chinese astrology. The signs are not based on the position of the stars as in Western astrology, but instead on the person's year of birth. Each animal is allocated its own years. There are 12 animals and they always appear in the same order (rat, ox, tiger, rabbit, dragon, snake, horse, goat, monkey, rooster, dog and pig). The cycle of animals, therefore, repeats itself every 12 years.

The Chinese calendar is based on the lunar year (orbits of the Moon around the Earth). The Western calendar is based on the solar year (orbit of the Earth around the Sun). The two do not correspond exactly. Each lunar year, therefore, begins on a slightly different date of the solar year.

To find your animal sign, look up the year of your birth in the first column of the following tables. If you were born in January or February of that year, however, remember to check the dates that the Chinese lunar year begins on, as you may find that you actually belong to the previous animal year. Once you have identified your animal sign, read the chapter devoted to that animal.

31 Jan 1900		–		17 Feb 1912	
1900	31 Jan 1900	–	18 Feb 1901		**Rat**
1901	19 Feb 1901	–	7 Feb 1902		**Ox**
1902	8 Feb 1902	–	28 Jan 1903		**Tiger**
1903	29 Jan 1903	–	15 Feb 1904		**Rabbit**
1904	16 Feb 1904	–	3 Feb 1905		**Dragon**
1905	4 Feb 1905	–	24 Jan 1906		**Snake**
1906	25 Jan 1906	–	12 Feb 1907		**Horse**
1907	13 Feb 1907	–	1 Feb 1908		**Goat**
1908	2 Feb 1908	–	21 Jan 1909		**Monkey**
1909	22 Jan 1909	–	9 Feb 1910		**Rooster**
1910	10 Feb 1910	–	29 Jan 1911		**Dog**
1911	30 Jan 1911	–	17 Feb 1912		**Pig**

18 Feb 1912		**–**	**4 Feb 1924**	
1912	18 Feb 1912	–	5 Feb 1913	**Rat**
1913	6 Feb 1913	–	25 Jan 1914	**Ox**
1914	26 Jan 1914	–	13 Feb 1915	**Tiger**
1915	14 Feb 1915	–	2 Feb 1916	**Rabbit**
1916	3 Feb 1916	–	22 Jan 1917	**Dragon**
1917	23 Jan 1917	–	10 Feb 1918	**Snake**
1918	11 Feb 1918	–	31 Jan 1919	**Horse**
1919	1 Feb 1919	–	19 Feb 1920	**Goat**
1920	20 Feb 1920	–	7 Feb 1921	**Monkey**
1921	8 Feb 1921	–	27 Jan 1922	**Rooster**
1922	28 Jan 1922	–	15 Feb 1923	**Dog**
1923	16 Feb 1923	–	4 Feb 1924	**Pig**

5 Feb 1924		**–**	**23 Jan 1936**	
1924	5 Feb 1924	–	24 Jan 1925	**Rat**
1925	25 Jan 1925	–	12 Feb 1926	**Ox**
1926	13 Feb 1926	–	1 Feb 1927	**Tiger**
1927	2 Feb 1927	–	22 Jan 1928	**Rabbit**
1928	23 Jan 1928	–	9 Feb 1929	**Dragon**
1929	10 Feb 1929	–	29 Jan 1930	**Snake**
1930	30 Jan 1930	–	16 Feb 1931	**Horse**
1931	17 Feb 1931	–	5 Feb 1932	**Goat**
1932	6 Feb 1932	–	25 Jan 1933	**Monkey**
1933	26 Jan 1933	–	13 Feb 1934	**Rooster**
1934	14 Feb 1934	–	3 Feb 1935	**Dog**
1935	4 Feb 1935	–	23 Jan 1936	**Pig**

24 Jan 1936		**– 9 Feb 1948**	
1936 24 Jan 1936	–	10 Feb 1937	**Rat**
1937 11 Feb 1937	–	30 Jan 1938	**Ox**
1938 31 Jan 1938	–	18 Feb 1939	**Tiger**
1939 19 Feb 1939	–	7 Feb 1940	**Rabbit**
1940 8 Feb 1940	–	26 Jan 1941	**Dragon**
1941 27 Jan 1941	–	14 Feb 1942	**Snake**
1942 15 Feb 1942	–	4 Feb 1943	**Horse**
1943 5 Feb 1943	–	24 Jan 1944	**Goat**
1944 25 Jan 1944	–	12 Feb 1945	**Monkey**
1945 13 Feb 1945	–	1 Feb 1946	**Rooster**
1946 2 Feb 1946	–	21 Jan 1947	**Dog**
1947 22 Jan 1947	–	9 Feb 1948	**Pig**

10 Feb 1948		**– 27 Jan 1960**	
1948 10 Feb 1948	–	28 Jan 1949	**Rat**
1949 29 Jan 1949	–	16 Feb 1950	**Ox**
1950 17 Feb 1950	–	5 Feb 1951	**Tiger**
1951 6 Feb 1951	–	26 Jan 1952	**Rabbit**
1952 27 Jan 1952	–	13 Feb 1953	**Dragon**
1953 14 Feb 1953	–	2 Feb 1954	**Snake**
1954 3 Feb 1954	–	23 Jan 1955	**Horse**
1955 24 Jan 1955	–	11 Feb 1956	**Goat**
1956 12 Feb 1956	–	30 Jan 1957	**Monkey**
1957 31 Jan 1957	–	17 Feb 1958	**Rooster**
1958 18 Feb 1958	–	7 Feb 1959	**Dog**
1959 8 Feb 1959	–	27 Jan 1960	**Pig**

	28 Jan 1960	–	**14 Feb 1972**	
1960	28 Jan 1960	–	14 Feb 1961	**Rat**
1961	15 Feb 1961	–	4 Feb 1962	**Ox**
1962	5 Feb 1962	–	24 Jan 1963	**Tiger**
1963	25 Jan 1963	–	12 Feb 1964	**Rabbit**
1964	13 Feb 1964	–	1 Feb 1965	**Dragon**
1965	2 Feb 1965	–	20 Jan 1966	**Snake**
1966	21 Jan 1966	–	8 Feb 1967	**Horse**
1967	9 Feb 1967	–	29 Jan 1968	**Goat**
1968	30 Jan 1968	–	16 Feb 1969	**Monkey**
1969	17 Feb 1969	–	5 Feb 1970	**Rooster**
1970	6 Feb 1970	–	26 Jan 1971	**Dog**
1971	27 Jan 1971	–	14 Feb 1972	**Pig**

	15 Feb 1972	–	**1 Feb 1984**	
1972	15 Feb 1972	–	2 Feb 1973	**Rat**
1973	3 Feb 1973	–	22 Jan 1974	**Ox**
1974	23 Jan 1974	–	10 Feb 1975	**Tiger**
1975	11 Feb 1975	–	30 Jan 1976	**Rabbit**
1976	31 Jan 1976	–	17 Feb 1977	**Dragon**
1977	18 Feb 1977	–	6 Feb 1978	**Snake**
1978	7 Feb 1978	–	27 Jan 1979	**Horse**
1979	28 Jan 1979	–	15 Feb 1980	**Goat**
1980	16 Feb 1980	–	4 Feb 1981	**Monkey**
1981	5 Feb 1981	–	24 Jan 1982	**Rooster**
1982	25 Jan 1982	–	12 Feb 1983	**Dog**
1983	13 Feb 1983	–	1 Feb 1984	**Pig**

2 Feb 1984	–	18 Feb 1996	
1984 2 Feb 1984	–	19 Feb 1985	**Rat**
1985 20 Feb 1985	–	8 Feb 1986	**Ox**
1986 9 Feb 1986	–	28 Jan 1987	**Tiger**
1987 29 Jan 1987	–	16 Feb 1988	**Rabbit**
1988 17 Feb 1988	–	5 Feb 1989	**Dragon**
1989 6 Feb 1989	–	26 Jan 1990	**Snake**
1990 27 Jan 1990	–	14 Feb 1991	**Horse**
1991 15 Feb 1991	–	3 Feb 1992	**Goat**
1992 4 Feb 1992	–	22 Jan 1993	**Monkey**
1993 23 Jan 1993	–	9 Feb 1994	**Rooster**
1994 10 Feb 1994	–	30 Jan 1995	**Dog**
1995 31 Jan 1995	–	18 Feb 1996	**Pig**

19 Feb 1996	–	6 Feb 2008	
1996 19 Feb 1996	–	7 Feb 1997	**Rat**
1997 8 Feb 1997	–	27 Jan 1998	**Ox**
1998 28 Jan 1998	–	5 Feb 1999	**Tiger**
1999 6 Feb 1999	–	4 Feb 2000	**Rabbit**
2000 5 Feb 2000	–	23 Jan 2001	**Dragon**
2001 24 Jan 2001	–	11 Feb 2002	**Snake**
2002 12 Feb 2002	–	31 Jan 2003	**Horse**
2003 1 Feb 2003	–	21 Jan 2004	**Goat**
2004 22 Jan 2004	–	8 Feb 2005	**Monkey**
2005 9 Feb 2005	–	28 Jan 2006	**Rooster**
2006 29 Jan 2006	–	17 Feb 2007	**Dog**
2007 18 Feb 2007	–	6 Feb 2008	**Pig**

THE FIVE ELEMENTS

Unlike Western astrology, Chinese astrology has five, and not four, elements. These are based on the five planets that were visible to the ancient Chinese astronomers. The elements are:

- water (ruled by Mercury)
- metal (ruled by Venus)
- fire (ruled by Mars)
- wood (ruled by Jupiter)
- earth (ruled by Saturn)

Each of these elements can manifest itself either positively or negatively. In the following tables, the negative and positive characteristics that each of the elements can bestow on a person are listed.

WATER

Positive	Negative
• artistic	• illogical
• expressive	• fearful
• nurturing	• stressed
• sensitive	• nervous
• understanding	• overly sensitive
• sympathetic	• subjective
• gentle	• manipulative
• caring	• fickle
• flexible	• passive
• unconfrontational	• dependent
• persuasive	• overimaginative

METAL

Positive	Negative
• protective	• inflexible
• visionary	• harsh
• prosperous	• longing
• resolute	• homesick
• inspirational	• self-righteous
• controlled	• single-minded
• determined	• competitive
• romantic	• solitary
• conviction	• cantankerous
• strength	• melancholic
	• opinionated

FIRE

Positive	Negative
• cheerful	• destructive
• passionate	• cruel
• honourable	• impatient
• loving	• tempestuous
• charismatic	• excessive
• dynamic	• reckless
• exciting	• demanding
• courageous	• radical
• decisive	• headstrong
• inventive	• exploitative
• optimistic	• ambitious

WOOD

Positive	Negative
● compassionate	● frustrated
● resourceful	● bad-tempered
● community minded	● impatient
● cooperative	● dissipated
● expansive	● unexpressive
● inspired	● excessive
● sociable	● violent
● extroverted	● angry
● problem solving	● pessimistic
● ethical	● temperamental
● practical	● susceptible

EARTH

Positive	Negative
● peaceful	● smothering
● methodical	● confining
● stable	● anxious
● patient	● pessimistic
● enduring	● slow
● just	● narrow-minded
● receptive	● rigid
● supportive	● overly cautious
● practical	● stubborn
● objective	● conservative
● logical	

Dominant element Each year is ruled by a different element. The element that rules a person's year of birth is called the dominant element. When you consider that every year is also ruled by one of the 12 animal signs, you can calculate that each combination of animal and element occurs only once every 60 years (12 x 5 = 60). For instance, the year 1901 was an ox/metal year. The next ox/metal year was 1961 and the next one will be in 2021. This is referred to as the 60-year cycle. According to the Chinese calendar, we are currently in the seventy-eighth cycle.

The natural elements and Yin and Yang

Animal	Yin/Yang	Natural element
rat	Yang	water
ox	Yin	water
tiger	Yang	wood
rabbit	Yin	wood
dragon	Yang	wood
snake	Yin	fire
horse	Yang	fire
goat	Yin	fire
monkey	Yang	metal
rooster	Yin	metal
dog	Yang	metal
pig	Yin	water

Natural element As well as this, each animal sign is considered to have its own, natural element. This is always the same regardless of a person's year of birth. The wheel below shows the natural element of each animal, as well as whether the animal is Yin or Yang. Yin and Yang are discussed overleaf. You will notice that only four (water, wood, metal and fire) of the five elements are natural elements.

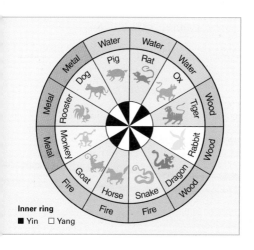

Inner ring
■ Yin   □ Yang

YIN AND YANG

According to Chinese philosophy, the whole universe is controlled by two primal forces. These are Yin and Yang. Everything can be categorized according to this system: from people to furniture, and even countries. The balance of the universe, the Earth, a nation and even the health and moods of individuals are determined by the balance or imbalance of Yin and Yang.

Yin and Yang symbol

The ideal balance of Yin and Yang is depicted by the symbol shown above. As the Yang part (white) decreases, the Yin part (black) increases; when one is at its height the other is at its lowest ebb. Often people assume that Yang is male and Yin female. This is not quite true. Although they are associated with opposite genders, each contains within itself the seed of the other. So, even though Yang is a masculine force, women can possess it. In such ways, Yin and Yang are opposing yet complementary principles. Neither is more important than the other and only together do they make a whole.

In the table below are listed some examples of Yin and Yang manifestations that show the opposing natures of these forces.

Yin	Yang
● Moon	● Sun
● dark	● light
● feminine	● masculine
● water	● fire
● black	● white
● passive	● active
● negative	● positive
● night	● day
● empty	● full
● cold	● hot
● no	● yes
● left	● right
● south	● north

Everyone has their own balance of Yin and Yang. To help you understand what makes you an individual, and your compatibility with other people, the tastes, colours, foods, flowers and plants associated with each animal sign are listed, together with the most auspicious seasons, time of birth and climate.

YIN AND YANG AND THE FIVE ELEMENTS

Each of the five elements has a positive and a negative side. Which of these is expressed in people depends on whether their animal sign is Yin or Yang. To work out if your animal sign is Yin or Yang, see the chart on pp. 18–19. For example, the rat is a Yang water animal. So, for rat people, the qualities of the element water are expressed positively. Pigs, on the other hand, are Yin water people. Therefore, the qualities of the element water express themselves negatively in pig people.

In the tables below and right are some of the qualities that are commonly attributed to people of either the Yin or Yang tendency.

Yin People	
● average weight or slender	● psychic
● often tall	● meditative
● smiling face	● intelligent
● like strong colours	● independent
● delicate health	● solitary
● individualist	● spiritual
● introspective	● rebellious
● responsive	● nonmaterialistic
	● introverted

COMPANION IN LIFE

The Chinese concept of the companion in life does not refer to another person, but rather to an inner person within an individual. This inner companion acts as a guide, guardian or devil's advocate. Your companion in life is

Yang People

- corpulent
- medium height
- healthy
- serious features
- self-preoccupied
- susceptible
- unstable emotionally
- fear failure
- confident
- conservative
- sociable
- hospitable
- optimistic
- active
- pragmatic
- efficient
- communally orientated
- distrustful
- materialistic
- passionate

determined by your hour of birth. Every two-hour slot of the day is governed by one of the 12 animal signs.

Identify your inner companion by referring to the table overleaf. Once you have established which of the animal signs is your inner companion, read the chapter devoted to that animal. Do not assume, however, that this means that you have the attributes of both the animal signs. Instead, your companion in life modifies the traits of your animal sign. For example, tigers are usually reckless and unpredictable people. A tiger whose inner companion is the ox, however, will be more stable than would otherwise be expected.

If a person has the same animal sign and inner companion, then they have the potential to balance the negative and positive aspects of their character.

Companion in life

The 24-hour cycle of the animals is shown in the table (right) and the diagrams. The hours given refer to local standard time. If you were born in a month when daylight saving or summer time were in use, you will need to deduct an hour (sometimes two) from your birth time before looking up the sign of your companion.

Time of birth	Sign of companion
11 pm – 1 am	Rat
1 am – 3 am	Ox
3 am – 5 am	Tiger
5 am – 7 am	Rabbit
7 am – 9 am	Dragon
9 am – 11 am	Snake
11 am – 1 pm	Horse
1 pm – 3 pm	Goat
3 pm – 5 pm	Monkey
5 pm – 7 pm	Rooster
7 pm – 9 pm	Dog
9 pm – 11 pm	Pig

THE COMPANION IN LIFE AND COMPATIBILITY

The compatibility of different animals can be radically altered by their respective companions in life. For example, horse and rat are naturally antagonistic towards each other. If the rat's companion in life is horse and the horse's companion in life is rat, however, then the reverse can be true.

WESTERN ASTROLOGY

To add an extra dimension to your Chinese astrological reading, you can consider it in conjunction with your Western zodiac sign.

The Western Zodiac	
22 December – 19 January	**Capricorn**
20 January – 18 February	**Aquarius**
19 February – 20 March	**Pisces**
21 March – 19 April	**Aries**
20 April – 20 May	**Taurus**
21 May – 20 June	**Gemini**
21 June – 22 July	**Cancer**
23 July – 22 August	**Leo**
23 August – 22 September	**Virgo**
23 September – 22 October	**Libra**
23 October – 21 November	**Scorpio**
22 November – 21 December	**Sagittarius**

Use the chart below to determine your Western star sign. There is a brief analysis of the effect of each star sign on an animal sign towards the end of each of the animal chapters.

More detailed information on Western astrology can be found in *Collins Gem Zodiac Types* which has a chapter devoted to each zodiac sign.

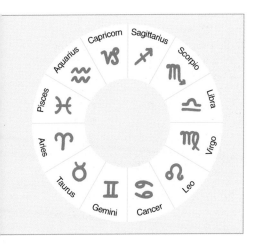

1. The Rat
The Yang water animal

Lunar years ruled by the rat					
1900	31 Jan 1900	–	18 Feb 1901
1912	18 Feb 1912	–	5 Feb 1913
1924	5 Feb 1924	–	24 Jan 1925
1936	24 Jan 1936	–	10 Feb 1937
1948	10 Feb 1948	–	28 Jan 1949
1960	28 Jan 1960	–	14 Feb 1961
1972	15 Feb 1972	–	2 Feb 1973
1984	2 Feb 1984	–	19 Feb 1985
1996	19 Feb 1996	–	7 Feb 1997

The rat was welcomed in ancient times as a protector and a bringer of material prosperity.

THE RAT PERSONALITY

Anxious not to be a failure, the affable, elegant and generous rat lives for today. When rat is being a charming socialite or a light-hearted gossip, this animal should never be underestimated. Attracted to whatever is clandestine, secretive or a potential bargain, the rat is a very clever animal who enjoys taking the best possible advantage of all situations.

CHARACTERISTICS

These are the general personality traits of those who are typical rats, both at their best and at their worst.

Positive	Negative
● intelligent	● calculating
● charming	● mean
● imaginative	● secretive
● placid	● restless
● opportunistic	● has ulterior motives
● passionate	● quick-tempered
● elegant	● a critical nit-picker
● sentimental	● a grumbler
● affectionate	● a gossip and a
● constructive critic	scandalmonger
● alert	● an obsessive
● honest	hoarder
● practical	● overambitious
● materialistic	● busybody
● quickly learns from	
experience	

SECRET RAT

Some rats suffer from a morbid guilt. Almost all fear failure so are often in a rat race. The rat's calm exterior hides inner aggressive restlessness. Rats tend to be gullible, falling into rat-traps, but they learn from experience so are constantly on guard.

ELEMENT

Rat is linked to the ancient Chinese element of water. Water endows rat with qualities of quiet restraint, persistence, diplomacy and the ability to predict future trends, especially in business and the material world. Water rats can influence others but need to turn their inner restlessness into active leadership.

BALANCE

The rat itself is Yang, but it is associated with the element water which is Yin, so rat people have a built-in potential for good balance. The Yin tendency of water, linked with night, darkness and introversion, can make good use of the resources of Yang, which is linked with day, light and extrovert initiative. For example, Yin has a natural inclination to respond to opportunities as they occur. Therefore, to thrive, rats have to work hard in response to situations not immediately under their control. This is stressful for rats, but their innate Yang tendency enables rats also to create opportunities for themselves, thus removing the stress and keeping labours to a minimum. Rats do not enjoy very hard work, especially that which is thrust upon them.

BEST ASSOCIATIONS

Traditionally, the following are said to be associated with rats:

Taste	salt
Season	winter
Birth	anytime in the summer
Colours	white, black, blue
Plants	savory, wormwood
Flowers	orchid, thistle
Food	peas, pork
Climate	cold

THE MALE RAT

If a man has a typical rat personality, he will generally display the behaviour listed below.

- attempts to profit from everyone
- has an alert eye for the best opportunities
- thrives on the rat race in his line of work
- lives by his wits
- has business acumen
- saves for his old age
- takes gambles
- enjoys spending money
- has a wide circle of acquaintances
- picks up gossip easily and hoards it
- is quick to calculate the odds in any situation
- is sentimental about his family
- has a very active imagination
- is suspicious of the ulterior motives of others
- is basically honest

THE FEMALE RAT

If a woman has a typical rat personality, she will generally display the behaviour listed below.

- rules the nest
- appears placid
- profits from her many acquaintances
- is a very resourceful businesswoman
- communicates well
- is an inveterate gossip
- has quick wits
- never misses a sale or a special offer
- keeps plenty of things in store
- is fashionable but always elegant
- is a superb homemaker
- rarely denies herself anything
- is passionate
- is direct and honest to a fault
- is intellectually creative
- is very good at getting other people working
- is generous to those she loves

THE RAT CHILD

If a child has a typical rat personality, he or she will generally display the behaviour listed below.

- is adventurous
- always takes things apart
- can't bear to be left out of anything
- will often be in trouble
- gets into fights
- will be able to get wants fulfilled
- is constantly busy
- embarrasses parents
- is into everything
- is happy and carefree
- loves exploring

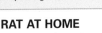

RAT AT HOME

Rats are not domestic people. They do, however, like to have somewhere that they can use rather like a retreat. The typical rat home is comfortable, well protected and well furnished. On special occasions, rats like to invite guests around. So a rat home will be a place fitted up for entertaining. Rats are good hosts and enjoy cooking for and entertaining guests. They are generous and have a flair for light-hearted pleasures. Rats like to enjoy the profits from their labours and are often sentimental at special times such as birthdays and anniversaries. Rats keep their homes tidy and are organized about chores.

If they live in a shared house, rats will be the ones to introduce a cleaning rota and a household kitty.

 ## RAT AT WORK

Rats have an aggressive drive that needs direction; they can be troublemakers if there is not enough to do. Although self-contained, rats can become neurotic about things at work. Rats need comfort and may seem lazy they prefer others to be doing the really hard work. No matter how much a rat earns, the money is often soon spent. Some rats get a reputation for being a bit of a crook, but this is only because they have an uncanny knack of making a profit out of any situation. Rats prefer to use their minds and their wits, rather than take part in any kind of physical labour.

Some typical rat occupations

- critic
- financial adviser
- broker
- moneylender
- lawyer
- detective
- antique dealer
- auctioneer
- connoisseur
- confidential situations
- songwriter
- pathologist
- underground work

RAT PREFERENCES

Likes

- entertaining
- oddities and the unusual
- being the first to explore new places
- underground passages
- mysteries
- unearthing solutions
- money
- taking a gamble
- company
- good-quality worldly possessions
- pleasure

Dislikes

- mundane everyday life
- alarm clocks
- rigid timetables
- agendas
- red tape
- bureaucracy
- having nothing to do
- any kind of failure
- being isolated

GOOD FRIENDS FOR RATS

The diagram below shows the compatibility of rat with other animals. There is no fixed ruling, however, because there are other influences on both the rat person and any potential friend. These influences are:

- the companion in life (see pp. 23–25)
- the dominant element (from the year of birth)

Compatibility of rat with other animals		
■ Rat	▲ Dragon	▲ Monkey
▲ Ox	● Snake	○ Rooster
■ Tiger	▼ Horse	● Dog
● Rabbit	○ Goat	● Pig

Key

▲ Highly compatible
● Amicable
■ No conflict but needs some effort
○ Lack of sympathy
▼ Antagonistic

Rat with rat This pairing can be very good or very bad. Two opportunistic rats can create double the trouble or double the benefit. At first, the relationship will be passionate but interest soon wanes when they finish exploring their similarities.

Ox with rat Even though these too have little in common, a match between them will be fortunate. Sensitive rat will appreciate ox's earnest nature. Ox will be attracted to rat's intelligence and sincerity. Rat can find a peaceful resting place with ox.

Tiger with rat The idealist tiger who doesn't care about material things and the materialist rat can be a good pair if they both make the effort. Together they could be volatile rebels with a cause, but rat will have to please tiger by letting tiger be the centre of attention.

Rabbit with rat Yes, these two can get along together very well, but rat should be careful not to exploit rabbit, which would spoil the friendship. Business partnerships will be more successful than romantic ones.

Dragon with rat This is a very good match. Both are easily bored so plenty of activity can be expected, although rat may have to let dragon take the dominant role. The rat will admire the dragon; as dragons love admiration, a relationship could work.

Snake with rat These two make a friendly pair who both enjoy fine things and will gossip together for hours. Snake can blow hot and cold and may be possessive one moment and wander off to new pastures the next, but all this will be temporary.

Horse with rat A relationship between these two egoists is definitely to be avoided unless there are very positive influences. Horse and rat really do rub each other up the wrong way. The lucid rat will be annoyed by the horse's excessive outbursts.

Goat with rat There is not much mutual understanding between these two but they are fine together for short periods for specific interests. In general, the carefree goat will be good for the rat, and will enjoy rat's charm.

Monkey with rat On the whole, this combination will last because they have much in common. They will make an entertaining but cunning pair, constantly hatching new plans. The relationship may be marred by competitiveness, however, and rat may have to accept monkey's dominance.

Rooster with rat These two have very little common ground for more than a passing acquaintance. No serious relationships are likely to develop unless there are other strong influences. Rats will judge roosters on appearance and find them vain and superficial.

Dog with rat On the whole, these two live in different worlds, so, while they can be quite friendly towards each other, the long-term prospects are not good because dog's passion for fair play will clash with rat's tendency to exploit.

Pig with rat This sensual pair can be very good friends for a while, but trusting pig is rather vulnerable to rat's charms and may end up unable to say no when necessary.

RAT IN LOVE

All is romance and passion when a typical rat falls in love. Rat will be as sentimental about little things shared together as about anniversaries. The love-partner of a rat can expect rat to be cautious and nervous at first until the relationship is better established, then rat's generosity will know no bounds. Rats are sensual people who will do much to please their partners. Unfortunately, once rats feel secure in a relationship, they have a tendency to be selfish and demanding. Unless they are strong-minded, rat partners may get depressed by this side of rat's nature.

 ## RAT AND SEX

Rat is not backward when it comes to making sexual advances. They like to take the initiative and favour exciting intrigues over safe affairs. Both male and female rats want sex in a romantic spot, or, even better, in a secret place. Rats offer frequent nights of mad, passionate love. Rats are naturally faithful and, if they stray, it is by chance and they will feel very guilty about it. If rat's partner is unfaithful, then rat will follow suit. The best way to seduce a rat is to find a setting for love that is secretive, mysterious and has candles and good wine. If you want rat to abandon you, set the scene for a boring evening in the most mundane, unromantic setting you can find. Rat will soon leave, blaming you for the split.

HEALTH

Rat's element, water, is associated in ancient Chinese acupuncture with the kidneys and bladder, so it is these organs that should be kept in good balance. The rat's tendency to hide anxieties could lead to an imbalance. The more rats learn to talk about their problems, the better for their general health.

LEISURE INTERESTS

Rat people are most likely to enjoy puzzles and games of chance. Following the stock market, keeping up with fashions and bargain-hunting for all kinds of antiques will please rat. Sports are not really rat's forte, except exploratory activities such as caving. Rats usually like to be associated with the current in-groups and enjoy all kinds of light-hearted socializing.

THE RAT YEARS AND THEIR ELEMENTS

The rat is a Yang water animal. Each of the rat years, however, is associated with an element which is said to have its own influence. These elements are wood, fire, earth, metal and water. They influence rat in a regular sequence, which is repeated every 60 years. In the table opposite, for example, the rat year 1900 is a metal year. The next metal year is 60 years later in 1960, and the next will be 2020.

Rat's natural element is water. When the year is a metal year, the influences of water and metal are said to be combined. Those born in the year of the rat 1960 are **Rat** *Water–Metal* people. The possible effects of the year elements are listed below.

Lunar years ruled by the rat and their elements			
1900	31 Jan 1900 –	18 Feb 1901	**metal**
1912	18 Feb 1912 –	5 Feb 1913	**water**
1924	5 Feb 1924 –	24 Jan 1925	**wood**
1936	24 Jan 1936 –	10 Feb 1937	**fire**
1948	10 Feb 1948 –	28 Jan 1949	**earth**
1960	28 Jan 1960 –	14 Feb 1961	**metal**
1972	15 Feb 1972 –	2 Feb 1973	**water**
1984	2 Feb 1984 –	19 Feb 1985	**wood**
1996	19 Feb 1996 –	7 Feb 1997	**fire**

Rat *Water–Metal* (1900, 1960)
This rat is endowed with integrity, ambition and the ability to make a sustained effort to carry a project through to its conclusion. On the negative side, metal can be too inflexible, leaning to rigid attitudes which threaten to stifle creative thought. This rat should try to be more malleable and open to compromise, although water does help to soften this tendency of metal.

Rat *Water–Water* (1912, 1972)
Rats born in water years are in their natural element. They are, therefore, doubly endowed with the ability to persuade diplomatically and have very acute awareness of future trends. On the negative side, the double water rat may become swamped with too much information and keep too much hidden in their watery depths. Atypically, water rats are very sensitive and are too concerned about the opinions of others. This rat should try to be more forthcoming and take the lead occasionally.

Rat *Water–Wood* (1924, 1984)
Wood is a creative element, so rats born in these years may be artistic in some way. They are also endowed with self-confidence, a strong moral sense and an ability to grow, expanding their activities widely. On the negative side, wood can create too many options, leading to a complexity that is unmanageable. Combined with indecisive water, this can mean trouble. These rats should try to control their inclination to bite off more than can be chewed and, instead, concentrate their resources.

Rat *Water–Fire* (1936, 1996)
This rat is endowed with decisiveness, wisdom and a capacity for innovation that leads to success. They can tolerate periods of rapid change and adjustment. On the negative side, they sometimes become too enthusiastic and passionate, which can lead to destruction of the very thing that they were about to achieve. This rat should try to control a sharp tongue and keep energies flowing in a positive direction.

Rat *Water–Earth* (1948, 2008)

Earth combined with water is a balancing combination for the rat. Earth rats are endowed with practicality, prudence, self-discipline and the ability to work hard. On the negative side, they may move too slowly, losing the initiative and delaying the taking of crucial decisions. This rat should use self-discipline to keep to a rigorously paced schedule, allowing the imagination more freedom.

RAT AND THE ZODIAC OF WESTERN ASTROLOGY

To work out your zodiac sign see pp. 26–27. General character traits of rats of the 12 zodiac signs are given below. Bear in mind that the Western zodiac sign modifies the basic rat nature – especially in the area of personal relationships.

Aries rat Independent, enthusiastic and original, this combination has great potential unless there is opposition, in which case Aries rat can be extremely aggressive. Aries' lack of stamina is balanced by rat's staying power.

Taurus rat Conservative, resourceful and artistically inclined, Taurean rats have great charm, love the good life but can be excessively indulgent. Taurus, however, will help rat to appreciate more fully the talents of others.

Gemini rat Social, great communicators and collectors of interesting ideas, these rats have a touch of magic and are quick-change artists. Having nothing to do is a disaster for Gemini rats and can lead to depression. Their quick wits will help them to achieve their ambitions.

Cancer rat These rats are very emotional, sensitive to the needs of others and protective. This combination can be overpowering and care should be exercised to keep things in perspective. Cancer rats, however, are great dreamers but have a good business sense.

Leo rat Dignified, optimistic and generous to a fault, Leo rats need to be in the limelight. This will have to be balanced with rat's preference for dark, secret places. These rats are great creative leaders, especially in the literary field.

Virgo rat Virgoan rats are meticulous, sensual and logical. This combination is excellent at painstaking research. The Virgo attention to detail and the rat desire to hoard can be put to excellent use in building reserves but these will never seem adequate.

Libra rat These rats are so charming, peaceable and refined that aggression almost never occurs. They are well balanced, diplomatic and value loyalty in personal relationships and in business. Libra rats seek companionship so are very romantic and must have music.

Scorpio rat Penetrative, investigative and passionate, Scorpio rats have accurate instincts and are aware of the darker side of human nature. These rats can become great criminologists or criminals. Others should be wary since these rats like to work alone.

Sagittarius rat Energetic, bluntly honest and disarmingly happy with life, these rats keep their sorrows and disappointments hidden. This combination can be successful in almost any project, provided variety and constant change are involved.

Capricorn rat Rats born under this sign are ambitious, controlling and difficult to change. The rat personality, however, helps them to loosen up and enjoy a little fun from time to time.

Aquarius rat Energetic Aquarius combines to make this rat very intellectual and an authority in several areas of research. A tendency to eccentricity can work wonders or lead to neuroticism, but it will ensure that life will never be dull for Aquarius rat.

Pisces rat An intuitive, well-intentioned and versatile combination, Pisces and rat can lead to confusion or the tendency to live in an illusory world. The rat's ability to gain from most situations, however, can result in success.

Some famous people born in the years of the rat and their zodiac signs

- **Lucrezia Borgia**
  Noblewoman
  18 Apr 1480 Aries

- **William Shakespeare**
  Playwright
  26 Apr 1564 Taurus

- **Wolfgang Amadeus Mozart**
  Composer
  27 Jan 1756 Aquarius

- **Jules Verne**
  Writer
  8 Feb 1828 Aquarius

- **Leo Tolstoy**
  Writer
  9 Sep 1828 Virgo

- **Auguste Rodin**
  Sculptor
  12 Nov 1840 Scorpio

- **Claude Monet**
  Artist
  14 Nov 1840 Scorpio

- **Mata Hari**
  Spy
  7 Aug 1876 Leo

- **Maurice Chevalier**
  Actor/Singer
  12 Sep 1888 Virgo

- **Spencer Tracy**
  Actor
  5 Apr 1900 Aries

- **Aaron Copland**
  Composer
  14 Nov 1900 Scorpio

- **Richard Nixon**
  USA President
  9 Jan 1013 Capricorn

- **Doris Day**
  Actress
  3 Apr 1924 Aries

- **Marlon Brando**
  Actor
  3 Apr 1924 Aries

- **Jimmy Carter**
  USA President
  1 Oct 1924 Libra

- **Charlton Heston**
  Actor
  4 Oct 1924 Libra

- **Yves St Laurent**
  Couturier
  1 Aug 1936 Leo

- **Vanessa Redgrave**
  Actress
  30 Jan 1937 Aquarius

- **Boris Spassky**
  Chessmaster
  30 Jan 1937 Aquarius

- **Prince Charles**
  Royalty
  14 Nov 1948 Scorpio

2. The Ox
The Yin water animal

Lunar years ruled by the ox			
1901	19 Feb 1901	–	7 Feb 1902
1913	6 Feb 1913	–	25 Jan 1914
1925	25 Jan 1925	–	12 Feb 1926
1937	11 Feb 1937	–	30 Jan 1938
1949	29 Jan 1949	–	16 Feb 1950
1961	15 Feb 1961	–	4 Feb 1962
1973	3 Feb 1973	–	22 Jan 1974
1985	20 Feb 1985	–	8 Feb 1986
1997	8 Feb 1997	–	27 Jan 1998

In China, many people do not eat beef as the ox is respected for the help it gives in working the land. The ox is associated with water and figures of oxen were once thrown into rivers to prevent flooding.

THE OX PERSONALITY

Basically, oxen are honest, straight-forward, kind-hearted people – often described as down-to-earth. Oxen have great reserves of strength to call on and are very hard-working. They are normally easy to get on with because they have no duplicity in them. Oxen do exactly what they say, and mean what they say. Despite being respectable and conventional, oxen are very independent-minded and not easily swayed by the opinions of others. They cannot take advice very well and can be intolerant and scathing to those they disagree with.

Positive	Negative
● conscientious	● slow
● patient	● stubborn
● hard-working	● intolerant
● reliable	● biased
● serious	● hot-tempered
● gentle	● dogmatic
● strong	● conservative
● careful	● materialistic
● persistent	● complacent
● determined	● conformist
● clear-thinking	● gloomy
● capable	● dull
● practical	

CHARACTERISTICS

These are the general personality traits of those people who are typical oxen, both at their best and at their worst.

SECRET OX

The image of the ox is that of a placid person. Mostly this is true. If, however, oxen are provoked or their patience stretched too far they can act like bulls shown a red rag. This hot-tempered side of ox's nature is well hidden but always present. Also, despite their homely images oxen are actually very innovative and creative people.

ELEMENT

Ox is linked to the ancient Chinese element of water. Water is linked to the arts and expressiveness. In oxen, however, water is more likely to be stagnant, and passively, rather than actively, expressed. Bear in mind, water can be both as nurturing as rain or as destructive as a hurricane.

BALANCE

Oxen value their privacy highly. They very rarely confide their feelings to anyone. Oxen go to great lengths to keep their innermost secrets and the barriers they build to protect themselves can become a prison. Unless people born in the year of the ox learn to balance this need for privacy with a more open and relaxed attitude to their emotions, they will become neurotic and suffer from self-delusion, as too much repression can direct the ox's quite formidable energies inward.

Traditionally, the following are said to be associated with oxen:

Taste	sweet
Season	winter
Birth	summer night
Colours	yellow, blue
Plant	hemp
Flower	orchid
Food	ginger
Climate	cold, wet

THE MALE OX

If a man has a typical ox personality, he will generally display the behaviour listed below.

- is difficult to understand
- keeps doubts to himself
- appears to be a pessimist
- values his family life
- plans ahead for the future
- is not particularly quick-witted
- is disciplined and dutiful
- has a tendency to be authoritarian
- loves good food and drink
- will be lazy at home
- is likely to be a chauvinist

THE FEMALE OX

If a woman has a typical ox personality, she will generally display the behaviour listed below.

- can be outspoken
- is lacking in the social graces
- is very good at organizing things
- is reticent but not shy
- will never forgive those who betray her
- is very industrious
- enjoys her home comforts
- is loyal to her family
- will always repay a debt
- is always dignified
- is a very private person
- is less inhibited than male oxen

THE OX CHILD

If a child has a typical ox personality, he or she will generally display the behaviour listed below.

- is best left alone when in a temper
- enjoys collecting things
- is serious and thoughtful
- has few close friends
- likes to make and build things
- is often a bookworm
- needs encouragement to relax
- enjoys own company
- will organize themselves

OX AT HOME

Oxen enjoy the material things in life. An ox home will be comfortable but not necessarily luxurious, as Oxen are practical people. They prefer to live in a rural area rather than a large city and the best location for an ox home is near water such as a river. If an ox is unable to live in the country, a garden is essential. It will be well maintained as oxen like to work with the earth and grow plants. If none of these options are possible, you are guaranteed to find many flourishing houseplants in an ox's home. An ox is likely to have a study or some area devoted to work in their house. It will be cluttered with old letters, photos, mementos and knick-knacks collected over the years. There will, of course, be some organizing system – but only the ox will understand it.

OX AT WORK

Oxen can achieve something in most professions as they will apply themselves and succeed through hard work and diligence. Before embarking on a project they have to first be interested and convinced of its worth, then they will explore all facets of the situation and finally decide on the best plan of action. In this calm and methodical way, logical oxen achieve a lot. They are, however, not suited to jobs that require negotiating skills. Working with food or in agriculture is often advantageous for an ox. Surprisingly, their ability to bring a carefully thought out and often highly unique solution to a problem makes oxen good candidates for the arts.

Some typical ox occupations

- composer
- landlord
- doctor
- religious leader
- estate management
- cook or chef
- police or military officer
- farmer
- soldier
- teacher
- philosopher
- judge
- banker
- insurance broker
- gardener

Oxen are suited to musical careers as they can apply themselves to the necessary practice as well as employ their creative capacities. As employers, oxen will be fair bosses and pay good wages but will expect loyalty to the company. As workers, oxen tend to blame others for their own mistakes. They are always punctual though.

OX PREFERENCES

Likes

- to save money
- home-cooked food
- the familiar
- to be appreciated
- sensible clothes
- traditional festivals such as Shrove Tuesday
- hand-made crafts
- sober or earthy colour schemes
- to plan ahead

Dislikes

- stressful occupations or pursuits
- fads and fashions
- change, especially if not voluntary
- novelties and gimmicks
- being taken for granted
- modern art
- heart-to-heart chats
- garish colours
- foolish or frivolous behaviour
- washing dirty linen in public

GOOD FRIENDS FOR OXEN

The diagram below shows the compatibility of ox with other animals. There is no fixed ruling, however, because there are other influences on both the ox and any potential friend. These influences are:

- the companion in life (see pp. 23–25)
- the dominant element (from the year of birth)

Compatibility of ox with other animals		
▲ Rat	▼ Dragon	■ Monkey
■ Ox	● Snake	▲ Rooster
▼ Tiger	○ Horse	○ Dog
▲ Rabbit	○ Goat	■ Pig

Key

▲ Highly compatible
● Amicable
■ No conflict but needs some effort
○ Lack of sympathy
▼ Antagonistic

Rat with ox A partnership between these two could be auspicious – it will be strong and fortunate. Sensitive rat will appreciate ox's earnest nature. Ox will be attracted to rat's intelligence and sincerity. Rat can find a peaceful resting place with ox.

Ox with ox Two oxen could be very happy together but one of them would have to make the first move. Otherwise the relationship would never get beyond acquaintanceship.

Tiger with ox Never! These two are natural enemies. Tiger's predilection for change and ox's need for orderliness do not go well together. There will definitely be arguments, fights even. Although tiger may seem more likely to dominate, ox will bulldoze tiger into defeat.

Rabbit with ox A harmonious match as rabbit likes to feel secure, and ox can provide security. Refined rabbit may find ox a little too homely and their straight-talking nature hard to handle.

Dragon with ox Wilful dragon is too much for most oxen to cope with. Any relationship between these two will not be long-lived. Ox enjoys daily routine; dragon is always trying to escape from it. If they can compromise, dragon may learn the value of taking time to reflect; ox could learn to appreciate the unusual.

Snake with ox Ox is dependable and will give ambitious snake the support he needs. Both like to work towards long-term goals. Each will respect the other's need for privacy and all should go well as long as snake does not reveal his manipulative nature to ox.

Horse with ox This will be an unhappy match for the pair. The two will only annoy each other. Lively horse will not get any excitement from ox; ox cannot give the flattery that vain horse requires. Also, horse is too free-thinking to accept ox's authoritarian habits for long.

Goat with ox Goat and ox have discordant personalities. Goat's habit of acting without thinking will only annoy careful ox. They also have different priorities in life: goat is too capricious and ox demands fidelity as the basis for a relationship.

Monkey with ox Mischievous monkey will tease serious ox, but usually gently and with love. Ox will be fascinated by monkey's sparkling personality but these two are unlikely to settle down together. They may misunderstand each other and monkey will not hang around long enough to sort any differences out.

Rooster with ox This is probably the best match for ox. These two are highly compatible. Sociable rooster complements ox's steady nature and ox will allow rooster to show off. They both care about money and financial security.

Dog with ox Imaginative dog may not be happy with staid ox. Dog is likely to criticize ox for lacking a sense of humour. If they can learn to respect each other, however, they can get along as both are realists and loyal.

Pig with ox Pig enjoys peace and quiet as much as ox but may find ox's responsible behaviour wearisome. Pigs like to go out and enjoy themselves; oxen like to stay at home and relax. Pig may find ox too demanding, ox will find pig irritating.

OX IN LOVE

Oxen are wary about falling in love. They know that it destroys routines and brings new and unfamiliar experiences. Oxen rarely lose their heads, let alone their hearts, over another. They appear to be dispassionate and unromantic because their forthright natures do not understand the subtleties and game-play of romantic entrapments. But do not be deceived; oxen are still capable of deep feelings and will be faithful, loving and devoted to their partners. Loyalty is very important to ox. Once betrayed they will find it hard to enter a new relationship. Ox will probably neglect anniversaries as ox is not particularly sentimental. Although oxen try not to be hurtful, they do need to learn how to respect their partner.

OX AND SEX

Oxen are usually considerate to others but can be timid in matters of love. They are unlikely to initiate love-making and find it hard to create a romantic atmosphere. Secretly, ox likes to be fussed over and even bossed around. Oxen are never jealous of their partner but will be jealous of their 'rights' – especially fidelity. Responsibility and trust are more important to an ox than good sex. Lovers of oxen can feel taken for granted, as physically undemonstrative ox can be clumsy and tongue-tied when it comes to expressing emotions. A subtle approach to them may not work as oxen cannot read between the lines. Furthermore, they will definitely be angered by outright criticism.

HEALTH

Ox's element, water, is associated with the kidneys, so ox should pay particular attention to keeping these organs in working order. Water is also associated with the ears and bladder. Drink plenty of water and do not allow your body to get lazy. Oxen should also guard against neuroses by learning to express their emotions.

LEISURE INTERESTS

Oxen enjoy exercise and like to keep themselves in shape. They prefer traditional sports – rugby, cricket or hockey, for example. Fighting sports are good for oxen as they allow them to vent their aggression in a controlled environment. Oxen are well suited to activities such as martial arts that require patience, practice and hard work to become skilled at.

For holidays, oxen do not like to travel more than they have to and definitely not alone. They are happier to go in a group. Nevertheless, oxen are capable of extremes and may decide to sail single-handedly around the world.

THE OX YEARS
AND THEIR ELEMENTS

The ox is a Yin water animal. Each of the ox years, however, is associated with an element which is said to have its own influence. These elements are water, fire, earth, metal and wood. They influence ox in a regular sequence, which is repeated every 60 years. In the table below, for example, the ox year 1901 is a metal year. The next ox metal year is 60 years later in 1961, and the next will be 2021. Ox's natural element is water; the influence of this combines with those of the element of the year of birth. The possible effects of the year elements are listed below.

Lunar years ruled
by the ox and their elements

1901	19 Feb 1901	– 7 Feb 1902	**metal**
1913	6 Feb 1913	– 25 Jan 1914	**water**
1925	25 Jan 1925	– 12 Feb 1926	**wood**
1937	11 Feb 1937	– 30 Jan 1938	**fire**
1949	29 Jan 1949	– 16 Feb 1950	**earth**
1961	15 Feb 1961	– 4 Feb 1962	**metal**
1973	3 Feb 1973	– 22 Jan 1974	**water**
1985	20 Feb 1985	– 8 Feb 1986	**wood**
1997	8 Feb 1997	– 27 Jan 1998	**fire**

Ox *Water–Metal* (1901, 1961)
Metal strengthens some of the ox's qualities, so metal oxen are even more stubborn and hard-working. They are also incredibly self-sufficient and resourceful. Conversely, metal also makes the ox less objective and more intuitive, while the ox's own strong character makes them the warmest of all metal people. Metal oxen are artistic and eloquent and they have both logic and vision. This produces charismatic people who inspire others with their inevitable achievements. These oxen can be domineering, however, and are prone to taking themselves too seriously.

Ox *Water–Water* (1913, 1973)

Water ox is in his natural element. Water brings sensitivity to this ox who is more likely to listen and help others. Atypically, this ox is almost diplomatic. Water helps oxen focus and channel their energies and water oxen find it easier to express their emotions. Therefore, they are less prone to neuroses. Although double water slows the ox down it also allows them to be more flexible. Despite being very patient, they are intolerant of weakness or self-pity in others.

Ox *Water–Wood* (1925, 1985)

The ox's natural water element allows the wood to flower. Wood oxen have physical strength combined with natural energy. They are the most innovative, creative and eloquent of all the oxen. These oxen have a better developed sense of humour and, at times, are even witty. Good learners, oxen born in a wood year are exceptional as they are not afraid to try new things. Wood makes this ox more sociable but due to its flammable nature also more quick-tempered.

Ox *Water–Fire* (1937, 1997)

Fire conflicts with water to produce an impatient ox who lacks the typical ox's placid approach to life. Fire oxen are combative and forceful characters. Although they often offend people, fire oxen do try not to cause unnecessary conflict. All oxen consider themselves superior to others, but they usually conceal this with modesty. Fire oxen, however, lack the ox's normal self-effacing manner and can appear proud and arrogant. In fact, they are basically kind and honest but lack the skills of tact and diplomacy.

Ox *Water–Earth* (1949, 2009)
The element earth is associated with many of the ox's innate qualities: reliability, resourcefulness, practicality, steadfastness and patience, for example. So these people are stereotypical oxen. Earth oxen are hugely materialistic but will always earn their wealth. They have a high sense of justice and are generous to those who need help. Earth allows the ox to be relatively at ease in expressing love physically. Earth oxen are the least creative of all oxen and they never take risks or short cuts. These people are very homely and pleasant but perhaps a little dull.

OX AND THE ZODIAC OF WESTERN ASTROLOGY

To work out your zodiac sign see p. 26–27. General character traits of oxen of the 12 zodiac signs are given below. Bear in mind that the Western zodiac sign modifies the basic ox nature – especially in the area of personal relationships.

Aries ox The combination of steadfast ox and volatile Aries makes these oxen both imaginative and persistent. They are interesting people who are both capable and spontaneous.

Taurus ox The bull and ox combine to accentuate the ox's character, good points and bad. They are very stable, reliable and down-to-earth, yet more tender. But these oxen must learn to be flexible.

Gemini ox These oxen are less serious then their counterparts. Relatively quick-witted, they are lively conversationalists but they can be too opinionated. Gemini oxen are very good company.

Cancer ox Cancer diminishes some of the ox's assets, such as reliability and determination. If they are not careful, Cancer oxen may never achieve their goals. Cancer can make the ox touchy but, deep down, they are very sensitive. These oxen are generally careful with money.

Leo ox Leo allows these people to get out of the traditional ox rut. They are more easy-going and fun-loving, unless opposed – Leonine oxen can be aggressive. Mostly, however, they are caring people and have great style.

Virgo ox Virgo brings precision to the patient ox, although others can find their perfectionism irritating and their manner too critical. Virgo oxen are often eccentrically conservative.

Libra ox Charming and popular, Libra oxen are at ease in social situations. They are sensual and love to indulge themselves. Atypically, these oxen don't mind talking about themselves; in fact, they feel a need to be understood.

Scorpio ox Ox determination combined with Scorpio depth make formidable characters who are still emotional and sensitive at heart. Dangerous when angry, however, they can be stubborn and are even violent at times. Scorpio oxen never compromise on anything.

Sagittarius ox Sagittarius brings balance to the ox. These oxen are the most open-minded of the breed. All oxen are given to reflection, but Sagittarian oxen go to the lengths of philosophizing.

Capricorn ox These people seek status, power and recognition. Eventually they will achieve them through perseverance. The most serious of all oxen, Capricornean ones do not suffer jokers.

Aquarius ox Ox born under this sign is more flexible than others. Aquarian oxen are very talkative but nervous and they find it hard to say what they really mean. Still powerful, they disguise their strength with subtlety.

Pisces ox An unlikely combination of flighty Pisces with steady ox produces a relatively frolicsome person. They are difficult to understand but are basically kind and loving. Piscean oxen should try a career in the arts.

Some famous people born in the years of the ox and their zodiac signs

- **J.S. Bach**
  Composer
  21 Mar 1685 Aries

- **Napoleon Bonaparte**
  Military leader
  15 Aug 1769 Leo

- **Antonín Dvořák**
  Composer
  18 Sep 1841 Virgo

- **Vincent van Gogh**
  Painter
  30 Mar 1853 Aries

- **William Butler Yeats**
  Poet/Playwright
  13 Jun 1865 Gemini

- **Charlie Chaplin**
  Comic actor
  16 Apr 1889 Aries

- **Adolf Hitler**
  Dictator
  20 Apr 1889 Taurus

- **Jawaharlal Nehru**
  Statesman
  14 Nov 1889 Scorpio

- **Walt Disney**
  Film producer
  5 Dec 1901 Sagittarius

- **Vivien Leigh**
  Actress
  5 Nov 1913 Scorpio

- **Paul Newman**
  Actor
  26 Jan 1925 Aquarius

- **Jack Lemmon**
  Actor
  8 Feb 1925 Aquarius

- **Margaret Thatcher**
  Politician
  13 Oct 1925 Libra

- **Warren Beatty**
  Actor/Director
  30 Mar 1937 Aries

- **Jack Nicholson**
  Actor
  28 Apr 1937 Taurus

- **David Hockney**
  Artist
  9 Jul 1937 Cancer

- **Dustin Hoffman**
  Actor
  8 Aug 1937 Leo

- **Robert Redford**
  Actor
  18 Aug 1937 Leo

- **Juan Carlos I**
  Spanish monarch
  5 Jan 1938 Capricorn

- **Meryl Streep**
  Actress
  22 Jun 1949 Cancer

3. The Tiger
The Yang wood animal

Lunar years ruled by the tiger			
1902	8 Feb 1902	–	28 Jan 1903
1914	26 Jan 1914	–	13 Feb 1915
1926	13 Feb 1926	–	1 Feb 1927
1938	31 Jan 1938	–	18 Feb 1939
1950	17 Feb 1950	–	5 Feb 1951
1962	5 Feb 1962	–	24 Jan 1963
1974	23 Jan 1974	–	10 Feb 1975
1986	9 Feb 1986	–	28 Jan 1987
1998	28 Jan 1998	–	5 Feb 1999

Associated with good fortune, power and royalty, tigers are viewed with both fear and respect. Their protection and wisdom is sought after. The Chinese see the tiger, and not the lion, as the king of animals.

THE TIGER PERSONALITY

Tigers are contrary creatures. The striped coat reflects tiger's ambivalent nature. Tigers are creatures of great strength and ability; but how this is used can vary greatly. They are born leaders or rebels, and instinctively protective, though prone to taking risks, so it may not always be wise to follow one. Often critical, tigers make fine revolutionaries. Once involved in battle, they usually come out on top, though their impetuosity can be their downfall.

CHARACTERISTICS

These are the general personality traits of those people who are typical tigers, both at their best and at their worst.

Positive	Negative
● loyal	● impetuous
● honourable	● disobedient
● wise	● arrogant
● protective	● impatient
● generous	● critical
● ambitious	● imprudent
● charismatic	● domineering
● daring	● aggressive
● fortunate	● selfish
● idealistic	● demanding
● courageous	● vain
● determined	● stubborn
● sensitive	● quarrelsome
● benevolent	

SECRET TIGER

On the surface, tigers may appear peaceful and controlled. Hidden underneath, however, there is often an aggressive and even belligerent nature. Also, surprisingly, when faced with difficult decisions, the seemingly decisive tiger has a tendency to retreat into procrastination.

ELEMENT

Tiger is linked to the ancient Chinese element of wood. The symbolism of wood is as ambivalent as that of the tiger. As a tree, wood's branches reach for the sky while its roots anchor it in the earth. This endows tiger with the ability (not necessarily used) to moderate his impulsive behaviour. Yet wood also gives the tiger passion, which can either lend gentleness to their behaviour or it may make them violent and destructive.

BALANCE

The tiger itself is Yang; its striped coat, however, represents the union of both Yin and Yang forces – the balance of which confers great power. It is this contradiction that is at the heart of understanding the nature of tigers. So, while tigers have huge potential, it is a potential for both success or failure. Although usually fortunate, tigers are predisposed to dangerous situations. If they act wisely, tigers can take advantage of this and become very successful. Otherwise, they may fail on a grand scale. Whether a tiger is calm and wise or impetuous and hot-headed in the use of power depends on the individual's ability to learn from experience and heed advice.

BEST ASSOCIATIONS

Traditionally, the following are said to be associated with tigers:

Taste	acid
Season	winter/spring
Birth	night
Colours	orange, dark gold
Plants	bamboo
Flowers	heliotrope
Food	bread, poultry
Climate	windy

THE MALE TIGER

If a man has a typical tiger personality, he will generally display the behaviour listed below.

- is good natured
- is peaceful in appearance
- is confident of his good fortune
- possesses a very strong will
- needs to achieve power and recognition
- gives good advice
- seeks attention
- is quick to take the lead
- is usually well mannered
- is a smart and elegant dresser
- takes risks
- is outspoken against authority
- often champions good causes
- is protective towards those weaker than himself
- is a passionate lover

THE FEMALE TIGER

If a woman has a typical tiger personality, she will generally display the behaviour listed below.

- is attracted to unusual places, things and people
- tries to be honest
- dislikes authority
- hates, and will fight against, injustice
- is intense in her feelings of love
- lives an adventurous life
- is not easily impressed by the fashionable
- is very good with children
- likes to be independent
- does not feel remorse or guilt easily
- is often a daring dresser
- will try to avoid the mundane in life
- is a good story-teller
- may be easy to offend
- is strong-spirited and intelligent
- can be demanding if she feels she is not valued
- is frank in her opinion of others
- tends to be authoritarian
- if bored, she will become aggressive and quarrelsome

THE TIGER CHILD

If a child has a typical tiger personality, he or she will generally display the behaviour listed below.

- is prone to accidents and injuries
- will not be a sneaky child
- likes school
- needs to experience a feeling of danger
- is difficult to discipline
- acts before thinking
- will probably be a constant source of worry
- likes to be the centre of attention
- is impatient and demanding
- will often get into scrapes
- is very energetic and playful
- likes to be treated maturely

TIGER AT HOME

A typical tiger home will be very comfortable. Probably expensive, furnishings will be tasteful and deceptively simple in design. Having a taste for the unusual, tiger's home may be decorated in a unique, though still elegant, fashion, perhaps decorated with mementos from travels abroad, for tigers like to roam and are not happy in one place for long. Tigers are not fond of housework, but, anxious to keep up appearances, they will do their chores quickly with the minimum of fuss. Dotted around the tiger's home you will probably find the odd trophy of some sporting, academic or other achievement. These are arrayed to impress guests.

TIGER AT WORK

Tigers are formidable business leaders. With their risk-taking natures and natural good luck, tigers make fine entrepreneurs. Tigers' creative minds are full of ideas of how to make money. Although they do not desire riches for their own sake, tigers love the chase. To be really successful, though, a tiger may need the steadying influence of another. Dragons make ideal business partners for tigers but a tiger will never be happy taking orders from someone else. This can create problems unless tiger's ego is regularly boosted. Even then, it won't take tigers long to work their way up the ranks to the top. Alternatively, tigers can often be found among the literary and artistic professions as noted writers, poets or artists, for example. As they yearn for recognition they may feel the need to communicate their ideas to others – usually with great success.

Some typical tiger occupations

- entrepreneur
- military officer
- head of state
- politician
- publicist
- musician
- writer/poet
- advertising executive
- designer
- film/theatre director
- stockbroker
- athlete
- film star
- trade union leader
- company director
- stunt person
- rebel leader
- explorer
- lion tamer
- teacher

TIGER PREFERENCES

Likes

- success
- to be their own person
- comfort, though not too sumptuous
- big parties
- appreciation and recognition of their prowess
- spending money
- honesty in others and themselves
- change and anything new or unusual
- to buy the best-quality goods they can afford
- a challenge
- being in charge
- flattery
- surprises

Dislikes

- failure
- feeling caged in by circumstances or people
- rules and laws made by others
- everyday life and its responsibilities
- paying attention to detail
- scandalmongering
- taking orders or criticism
- nursing others
- jewels and trinkets
- being ignored
- established authority

GOOD FRIENDS FOR TIGERS

The diagram below shows the compatibility of tiger with other animals. There is no fixed ruling, however, because there are other influences on both the tiger and any potential friend. These influences are:

- the companion in life (see pp. 23–25)
- the dominant element (from the year of birth)

Also, for any relationship to succeed, the tiger must be the centre of attention and at least appear to take the lead.

Compatibility of tiger with other animals		
■ Rat	▲ Dragon	▼ Monkey
▼ Ox	○ Snake	○ Rooster
■ Tiger	▲ Horse	▲ Dog
● Rabbit	■ Goat	● Pig

Key

▲ Highly compatible
● Amicable
■ No conflict but needs some effort
○ Lack of sympathy
▼ Antagonistic

Rat with tiger Although both passionate, the idealistic tiger and the materialistic rat can only be a good pair if they both make the effort. Tiger may find rat charming but a little insincere. Rat may be impressed by tiger's energy but will not appreciate his impulsiveness.

Ox with tiger Tiger's predilection for change and ox's need for orderliness do not go well together. In fact, their temperaments are so different that these too are often enemies.

Tiger with tiger Any relationship between two tigers will be fiery. During good times, the tigers' love of excitement and basic good nature will make for a wild relationship. They will not be able to stand each other, however, during bad times. Ultimately, as all tigers need to be the centre of attention, two tigers is often one too many.

Rabbit with tiger Basically these two understand each other very well. Rabbit is tactful enough to let tiger take the lead. Sometimes, however, rabbit will not take tiger seriously, and tiger will resent this. If the two share an interest, the bond will be stronger.

Dragon with tiger Very similar in temperament, both are impulsive and passionate, yet dragon provides a steadying influence on tiger. Any relationship between them will never be boring. As they are both frank, misunderstandings do not last for long.

Snake with tiger Snake and tiger approach life from opposite angles. Snake follows its head and tiger its heart; snake likes peace and quiet while tiger likes action and risk. Both would misunderstand, and feel suspicious of, the motivations of the other.

Horse with tiger There can be great attachment between a tiger and a horse. Patient horse will enjoy the company of energetic tiger and stick by tiger when he's down. Even so, they will probably still argue and need to take time out from the relationship occasionally.

Goat with tiger A difficult but potentially mutually rewarding partnership. Goat will admire tiger's nerve and loyalty while tiger will appreciate goat's fun-loving nature. To be more than fair-weather friends, however, a little effort will be needed.

Monkey with tiger Tiger and monkey are both competitive and neither knows how to compromise. Secretly monkey may admire, but cannot resist mocking, tiger; tiger cannot help retaliating, and the relationship could quickly become destructive. Unless there is great love on monkey's part and moderation on tiger's part, no relationship will work.

Rooster with tiger Initially promising, tiger and rooster are unable to have more than a brief friendship. Although these two colourful characters have much in common, they will quickly fall to misunderstanding and criticizing each other. Not given to reflection, tiger will most likely fail to see the thoughtful nature behind rooster's swaggering facade.

Dog with tiger The different natures of these two actually complement each other perfectly. Anxious dog will curb tiger's excessive risk-taking; tiger will appreciate dog's loyalty. The relationship could prove long-lasting and stable. Both are idealists, and can combine their talents to achieve great things for a good cause.

Pig with tiger These two can get on well together as they are both gregarious, tolerant and independent. Tiger will protect pig from his enemies and pig will prove loyal. Be warned, however, that tiger may be tempted to test pig's temper and find himself at the losing end.

TIGER IN LOVE

Thanks to their charismatic personalities, tigers are not short of admirers. Led by the heart, tiger is quick to fall in love. When in love, tiger will at first be intense and passionate. After the initial thrill has passed, however, tiger often loses interest. Therefore the love life of a tiger may be hard to keep up with – full of ups and downs, bursts of passion and many 'conquests'. If tiger's love-partner is clever, they will let tiger know that they would be quite happy alone. This will ensnare tiger, who hates an easy prey. Tiger can make a romantic, affectionate but sometimes inattentive partner.

TIGER AND SEX

Tiger's boundless energy, creative mind and passionate nature make both the male and female imaginative and energetic lovers. Lovemaking will most likely come in short bursts as tigers are sprinters, not long-distance runners. To seduce a tiger, remember that luxurious or exotic settings are best; a touch of danger added to the encounter will be an irresistible lure. On the whole, tigers are faithful; if they do have an affair it will be to assert their independence. Tigers expect loyalty from their mates, so if the tiger's partner is unfaithful, the relationship will soon end. To get rid of unwanted tigers, don't ignore them! Simply become possessive, demanding, dependent – make them feel caged in and they'll soon break away.

HEALTH

Tiger's element, wood, is associated with the liver, so tigers should pay particular attention to keeping this organ in working order. Emotionally, tiger should let off steam occasionally by releasing any pent-up anger or passion. Otherwise tiger may become too anxious and obsessive.

LEISURE INTERESTS

Tiger people tend to engage in the more energetic and daring varieties of any activity. So skiing, hang-gliding, stock-car racing or surfing are ideal sports for the tiger. For their holidays, tigers like to travel to distant places. Package tours, though, are not their style; trekking, mountaineering, going on safaris, white-water rafting and so on are more suitable. On a tamer level, tigers love a good party where they can cause a stir.

THE TIGER YEARS AND THEIR ELEMENTS

The tiger is a Yang wood animal. Each of the tiger years, however, is associated with an element which is said to have its own influence. These elements are wood, fire, earth, metal and water. They influence tiger in a regular sequence, which is repeated every 60 years. In the table below, for example, the tiger year 1902 is a water year. The next tiger water year is 60 years later in 1962, and the next will be 2022. Tiger's natural element is wood; the influence of this combines with those of the element of the year of birth. The possible effects of the year elements are listed below.

Lunar years ruled
by the tiger and their elements

1902	8 Feb 1902	– 28 Jan 1903	**water**
1914	26 Jan 1914	– 13 Feb 1915	**wood**
1926	13 Feb 1926	– 1 Feb 1927	**fire**
1938	31 Jan 1938	– 18 Feb 1939	**earth**
1950	17 Feb 1950	– 5 Feb 1951	**metal**
1962	5 Feb 1962	– 24 Jan 1963	**water**
1974	23 Jan 1974	– 10 Feb 1975	**wood**
1986	9 Feb 1986	– 28 Jan 1987	**fire**
1998	28 Jan 1998	– 5 Feb 1999	**earth**

Tiger *Wood–Water* (1902, 1962)

This reserved tiger is endowed with compassion and is more sensitive to the needs of others than a typical tiger. Full of noble ideas, combined with an ability to control passionate whims and look before leaping, this tiger can make a just and wise leader. A water tiger's life will be more calm than other tigers'. There is a tendency, though, for water tigers to be slightly pompous.

Tiger *Wood–Wood* (1914, 1974)

This sociable tiger is particularly charming and witty – a real party animal. Wood tigers are very enterprising and good at thinking up grand schemes; the details, however, will be left to others to sort out. Apparently superficial emotionally, double wood tigers can actually become quite anxious – so they should try to keep stress under control.

Tiger *Wood–Fire* (1926, 1986)

Tigers are already inherently Yang; fire is also Yang. This doubling of the Yang force makes fire tigers incredibly active people. They are animated, exciting yet changeable characters. Sensitive to perceived slights, the fire tiger often has a very quick temper and can soon become explosive. Fortunately, bursts of temper never last long with this tiger. To really enjoy life, fire tiger needs to try and relax and take things at a more controlled pace.

Tiger *Wood–Earth* (1938, 1998)

Unlike most other tigers, earth tiger is hardly impulsive at all, naturally less excitable and not averse to stability and continuity. This tiger is very practical and fond of comfort. For such reasons, earth tigers tend to be more successful at long-term relationships than other tigers. There is a danger, however, that unless they give free rein to their dynamic Yang element, earth tigers can become real stick-in-the-muds. This should be avoided, and instead a more outward-looking mind should be cultivated.

Tiger *Wood–Metal* (1950, 2010)
This tough, outspoken tiger can sometimes be too bossy. Metal tiger is less ruled by the heart than typical tigers. Unfortunately, sometimes this only serves to make them unscrupulous. Metal tigers can be high achievers as they are very ambitious and self-disciplined. Advice to a metal tiger would be to try to listen to the wishes of others, practise tact and be more flexible.

TIGER AND THE ZODIAC OF WESTERN ASTROLOGY

To work out your zodiac sign see p. 26–27. General character traits of tigers of the 12 zodiac signs are given below. Bear in mind that the Western zodiac sign modifies the basic tiger nature – especially in the area of personal relationships.

Aries tiger This is the most reckless and impetuous of all tigers. Aries tiger is well loved for sincerity, frankness and kind-heartedness. Although not very reflective, Aries tiger is very talented and often conscientious.

Taurus tiger Careful but bold, a realist but brave, passionate but reliable, Taurus tiger combines the attributes of these two signs to great effect. This tiger is practical and determined, so will often achieve great material prosperity.

Gemini tiger Impulsive tiger and mercurial Gemini make this person a mental and physical nomad. Hard to pin down to one idea or place, Gemini tigers are nonetheless highly creative people. What they lack in stamina, they make up for with inventiveness.

Cancer tiger The combination of these opposites makes an enigmatic and at times overly sensitive person. Cancer tigers are often eccentric but likable characters. Self-discipline is vital to ensure that tasks are achieved, as Cancer tigers have a tendency for introspection.

Leo tiger Both Leos and tigers seek the limelight, a Leo tiger doubly so. Also, the Leo tiger is naturally arrogant, so at times this tiger can be unbearable. Nevertheless they are generous, loyal and charming people as well.

Virgo tiger Hesitant Virgo and foolhardy tiger actually go very well together. A Virgo tiger is trustworthy, self-disciplined, diligent and resourceful – an unbeatable combination. On the negative side, this variety of tiger may be a snob.

Libra tiger Noble tiger's sense of justice is enhanced by the altruistic Libran sign. Libra tigers are often very attractive personalities. They combine a hard-working trait with a charming and compassionate nature.

Scorpio tiger These tigers display all the tiger traits in the extreme; they have fearsome tempers, huge amounts of energy and are dangerously reckless. As a friend, loyal

Scorpio tiger is a great advantage; as an enemy, beware!

Sagittarius tiger The Sagittarian tiger is an unpredictable dreamer. Basically gentle and easy-going, they can at times be infuriatingly changeable. Perhaps extroverted then withdrawn, generous then miserly – these people do not like to be taken for granted.

Capricorn tiger Capricorn endows these tigers with the ability to avoid their usual pitfalls – in particular thoughtlessness. Capricorn tigers are not as at ease socially as others, though, and tend to be moody. They are, however, dependable and good-natured.

Aquarius tiger This is the most idealistic of tigers. Intellectual Aquarius complements active tiger well; great things could be accomplished. Gullibility and lack of steadfastness can prove a problem. Aquarian tigers are fascinated by the latest gadgets.

Pisces tiger This tiger is sympathetic, loving, very creative but often woefully indecisive. The Pisces tiger will only achieve inner peace when the tiger is fully under control.

Some famous people born in the years of the tiger and their zodiac signs

- **William Wordsworth**
  Poet
  7 Apr 1770 Aries

- **Karl Marx**
  Social philosopher
  5 May 1818 Taurus

- **Emily Brontë**
  Novelist
  30 July 1818 Leo

- **Oscar Wilde**
  Writer
  16 Oct 1854 Libra

- **H G Wells**
  Writer
  21 Sep 1866 Virgo

- **Ho Chi Minh**
  Political leader
  19 May 1890 Taurus

- **Agatha Christie**
  Writer
  15 Sep 1890 Virgo

- **Groucho Marx**
  Comedian
  2 Oct 1890 Libra

- **Dwight D. Eisenhower**
  US President
  14 Oct 1890 Libra

- **Charles de Gaulle**
  French President
  22 Nov 1890 Sagittarius

- **John Steinbeck**
  Novelist
  27 Feb 1902 Pisces

- **Georgette Heyer**
  Novelist
  16 Aug 1902 Leo

- **Alec Guinness**
  Actor
  2 Apr 1914 Aries

- **Dylan Thomas**
  Poet/Writer
  27 Oct 1914 Scorpio

- **Hugh Hefner**
  Publisher
  9 Apr 1926 Aries

- **Queen Elizabeth II**
  Monarch
  21 Apr 1926 Taurus

- **Marilyn Monroe**
  Actress
  1 June 1926 Gemini

- **Joan Sutherland**
  Opera singer
  7 Nov 1926 Scorpio

- **Rudolf Nureyev**
  Ballet dancer
  17 Mar 1938 Pisces

- **Germaine Greer**
  Feminist
  29 Jan 1939 Aquarius

4. The Rabbit
The Yin wood animal

Lunar years ruled by the rabbit

1903	29 Jan 1903	–	15 Feb 1904
1915	14 Feb 1915	–	2 Feb 1916
1927	2 Feb 1927	–	22 Jan 1928
1939	19 Feb 1939	–	7 Feb 1940
1951	6 Feb 1951	–	26 Jan 1952
1963	25 Jan 1963	–	12 Feb 1964
1975	11 Feb 1975	–	30 Jan 1976
1987	29 Jan 1987	–	16 Feb 1988
1999	6 Feb 1999	–	4 Feb 2000

The rabbit is associated with longevity and the moon. Some astrologers identify this sign as the cat, not rabbit, but Chinese astrologers always refer to it as the rabbit or hare.

THE RABBIT PERSONALITY

Seemingly unexceptional, rabbits provoke extreme reactions. They inspire either adoration or hate, but never indifference. Rabbits are mysterious yet practical, timid but ruthless, articulate but inscrutable, and virtuous as well as cunning. They like their lives to be secure, comfortable and calm, yet they are fiercely independent. Sensitive and intuitive by nature, rabbits are easily influenced by their emotions.

CHARACTERISTICS

These are the general personality traits of those people who are typical rabbits, both at their best and at their worst.

Positive	Negative
● diplomatic	● indecisive
● circumspect	● unpredictable
● peaceful	● hesitant
● sensitive	● faint-hearted
● intuitive	● easily shocked
● discreet	● touchy
● moderate	● conservative
● reflective	● conformist
● well-organized	● egotistical
● principled	● superficial
● refined	● cruel
● hospitable	● gossipy
● intelligent	● cunning
● expressive	● secretive
● honourable	● pedantic

SECRET RABBIT

People often assume that rabbits' need for security and comfort combined with the urge to avoid confrontation means that they are weak. This is not true. Rabbits will use all their diplomacy, charm and cunning to achieve their ends. The fact that they very rarely need to resort to outright battle to get their own way is proof of rabbits' strength, not weakness, of character.

ELEMENT

Rabbit is linked to the ancient Chinese element of wood. Wood can be both flexible like a sapling or sturdy as an oak. How its energy is expressed depends on how well a wood person can both control and indulge their natural tendencies. For a rabbit, the tendencies to be watched are the urge to avoid change or trouble at all costs, self-indulgence and timidity.

BALANCE

The behaviour of a rabbit can be unpredictable as it varies according to current circumstances. During peaceful times, rabbits will be at ease and relaxed. Sudden changes, unforeseen events or conflicts will unbalance rabbits and make them irritable, confused, and even aggressive. Rabbit people will not be happy at such times until they are back in control of the situation. Also, rabbit personalities need to balance their self-preoccupied Yin natures and occasionally try to see things from another's point of view.

BEST ASSOCIATIONS

Traditionally, the following are said to be associated with rabbits:

Taste	acid
Season	spring
Birth	summer
Colours	white
Plant	fig tree
Flower	Queen Anne's lace
Food	wheat, poultry
Climate	windy

THE MALE RABBIT

If a man has a typical rabbit personality, he will generally display the behaviour listed below.

- is not a victim of fashions
- is careful when spending money on necessities
- is extravagant with his money when buying luxuries
- is neat and well dressed
- has a tendency to be superficial
- is interested in the arts and culture
- is not a family-minded man
- is faithful and loving
- is a careful listener
- is happy and content
- has a traditional outlook
- is protective towards his peace and quiet
- is flamboyant
- is in touch with his feminine side but not effeminate

THE FEMALE RABBIT

If a woman has a typical rabbit personality, she will generally display the behaviour listed below.

- is not overtly maternal
- is good at entertaining
- is sophisticated
- is tender and wistful
- is very determined
- is good at giving practical advice
- makes herself at home in most social circles
- is attentive to her material needs
- is able to strike a good bargain
- is naturally elegant and always stylishly dressed
- is wary of commitment
- has a sharp sense of humour
- is emotional
- prefers a comfortable to an adventurous life
- can be manipulative to get her own way
- prefers company to solitude
- is well mannered and conscious of etiquette

THE RABBIT CHILD

If a child has a typical rabbit personality, he or she will generally display the behaviour listed below.

- is unargumentative
- is shy and sometimes nervous
- is obedient and well disciplined
- is happy at school
- enjoys team sports
- is usually more academic than athletic
- needs stimulation and motivation
- can be lacking in imagination
- is prone to nightmares
- succeeds through hard work
- enjoys fairytales and fantasy stories

RABBIT AT HOME

Rabbits are sensitive to environments and like to create cosy, intimate homes. Furnishings will be beautiful and comfortable; antiques or classic designs are preferred. Rabbits are meticulous and cannot bear to have an untidy or unclean home; a spill of red wine could move a rabbit to hysteria. Rabbits prefer to entertain at home rather than venture out into the cold. They make fine hosts and hostesses as they go to great lengths to make guests feel at home. Rabbits put a lot of effort into arranging their environments. Once established and satisfied with their homes, rabbits hate the disruption of moving house.

RABBIT AT WORK

Although rabbits are not authoritative, they can make good leaders and organizers as they are skilled diplomats. A rabbit can win a battle without anyone knowing one has been fought. Not being ambitious, rabbits rarely reach the top of their chosen professions. They excel in administrative or clearly defined positions. Once rabbits know what needs to be done, they are thorough and diligent in carrying out their tasks. They are good at team work, but often prefer to work alone or be self-employed. Job security is important, so stable professions are preferred. With their ability to charm, rabbits are good at wheeling and dealing. However, their basically honest nature stops them from taking too much advantage of this. In business, rabbits should try and use their instinctive good taste, careful nature and ability to evaluate a situation well to good advantage.

Some typical rabbit occupations

- antique dealer
- diplomat
- administrator
- interior decorator
- politician
- historian
- art collector
- barrister

- tailor
- receptionist
- chemist
- landlord
- pharmacist
- beautician
- accountant
- librarian

RABBIT PREFERENCES

Likes

- privacy
- conversation, including gossip
- to have a routine
- to use their wits to solve a problem
- romantic films
- secrets and mysteries
- long hairstyles
- prefers company of good friends and family to going out
- comfortable surroundings
- beautiful paintings
- paying attention to detail

Dislikes

- arguments
- to see or use violence
- drastic change
- taking risks
- surprises
- to say anything unpleasant
- being forced to make a decision
- complicated plans
- to change their mind
- commitment
- open criticism

GOOD FRIENDS FOR RABBITS

The diagram below shows the compatibility of rabbit with other animals. There is no fixed ruling, however, because there are other influences on both the rabbit and any potential friend. These influences are:

- the companion in life (see pp. 23–25)
- the dominant element (from the year of birth)

Compatibility of rabbit with other animals

● Rat	○ Dragon	○ Monkey
▲ Ox	▲ Snake	▼ Rooster
■ Tiger	▼ Horse	● Dog
■ Rabbit	▲ Goat	● Pig

Key

▲ Highly compatible
● Amicable
■ No conflict but needs some effort
○ Lack of sympathy
▼ Antagonistic

Rat with rabbit These two can get on very well. Rabbit should make sure, however, that rat does not exploit the relationship. Business partnerships will be more successful than romantic ones.

Ox with rabbit An ideal match, ox can provide rabbit with security and peace so that the two can live in harmony. Rabbit may find ox's straight-talking nature hard to handle, and at times may be tempted to stray to assert their independence.

Tiger with rabbit Unexpectedly, these two actually understand each other very well. Perhaps too well for a lasting relationship, as rabbit has a tendency not to take tiger seriously.

Rabbit with rabbit Two rabbits can live together without ever arguing. Rabbits can be too passive, so the relationship may lack in excitement unless one of them is a bit more adventurous.

Dragon with rabbit Unlikely to get on, dragons annoy rabbits with their madcap, untidy natures. A compromise could be achieved if both have their own space.

Snake with rabbit Both snakes and rabbits cultivate peace and security, and share a love of the arts. Snake can help rabbit be more adventurous, as long as rabbit is tolerant of snake's less virtuous nature.

Horse with rabbit Moody horse makes a disruptive partner for rabbit, who may not tolerate this for long unless very much in love.

Goat with rabbit This may be the best match as both have good taste and a love of luxuries. Goat's imaginative nature appeals to rabbit's romantic side. In difficult times, however, neither will be able to look to the other for courage and support as both are anxious creatures.

Monkey with rabbit Devious monkey can bring out the worst, cunning side of rabbit. But, as lively monkey finds stable rabbit dull, they are not often together long enough for this to happen.

Rooster with rabbit On no account should these two attempt a serious relationship. Rooster's tendency to voice criticisms will send rabbit running, and rooster will find rabbit unsympathetic.

Dog with rabbit Loyal dog gets on well with rabbit and the two can have a happy relationship, as long as they do not take each other for granted.

Pig with rabbit Pleasure-loving, tolerant pig is a good match for rabbit. Discreet rabbit may be a bit unnerved by sensual pig's public displays of affection, but this is a minor point.

RABBIT IN LOVE

Rabbits are wary of commitment as it involves change and making a major decision. This does not mean that they are fickle, just careful about choosing their partners. Rabbits would rather be alone than in unsatisfactory relationships; they prize their peaceful lives highly. Once committed, rabbits put a lot of effort into their relationships. Always willing to listen and loathe to argue, they make attentive, tender and loving partners. Despite this, it is sometimes hard to know what rabbit partners are feeling or thinking as they are very private people. Rabbits listen better than they confide. This can be exasperating for others unless they learn how to read the signs. Rabbits need a lot of attention and love – but most are clever enough to have learnt that, if given, these will be returned.

RABBIT AND SEX

Not quick to jump into bed, courtships are lengthy with rabbits and it may be left to others to take the initiative. Once involved, a rabbit will be a faithful lover. Traditional and sensitive by nature, rabbits are often romantics and are easily seduced by roses, candlelit dinners and perhaps even poetry if it is not avant-garde. But do not assume that they will appreciate drama in their sex life – sophisticated rabbits are repulsed by raw emotion and tears. Rabbits can be unexciting lovers as they are inhibited people and restrained by their lack of imagination. They do listen well, however, and like to please, so a rabbit will be willing to learn what their partner likes in bed. If still a bit hesitant, try being demanding as rabbits hate confrontation and will do most things for a quiet life. Nothing kinky will be tolerated though, as rabbits are actually quite prudish.

HEALTH

Rabbit's element, wood, is associated with the liver, so rabbits should pay particular attention to keeping this organ in working order. Rabbits should make sure that they get enough exercise, otherwise their love of a quiet, comfortable life could damage their long-term health. Psychologically, rabbits need to try and not be too self-absorbed and over-concerned with themselves. Also, they should take care that their methodical, tidy natures do not become obsessively fastidious.

LEISURE INTERESTS

Rabbits will enjoy a wide range of activities, as long as they are not responsible for organizing them. For this reason, package tours are well suited to rabbits. Although not especially sporty, they can make good team players. Being lovers of art and culture, rabbits can often be found visiting museums and art galleries. Even though they are usually music lovers, rabbits would rather listen to a good recording in the comfort of their own home than go to a crowded, live concert. Rabbits like to be alone at times and may go on long nocturnal walks to indulge this. Great lovers of the good things in life – fine wine, gourmet food and conversation – rabbits like to throw dinner parties for friends. Entertaining at home is always preferred to wild parties.

THE RABBIT YEARS AND THEIR ELEMENTS

The rabbit is a Yin wood animal. Each of the rabbit years, however, is associated with an element which is said to have its own influence. These elements are wood, fire, earth, metal and water. They influence rabbit in a regular sequence, which is repeated every 60 years. In the table overleaf, for example, the rabbit year 1903 is a water year. The next rabbit water year is 60 years later in 1963, and the next will be 2023. Rabbit's natural element is wood; the influence of this combines with those of the element of the year of birth. The possible effects of the year elements are listed below.

**Lunar years ruled
by the rabbit and their elements**

1903	29 Jan 1903	– 15 Feb 1904	**water**
1915	14 Feb 1915	– 2 Feb 1916	**wood**
1927	2 Feb 1927	– 22 Jan 1928	**fire**
1939	19 Feb 1939	– 7 Feb 1940	**earth**
1951	6 Feb 1951	– 26 Jan 1952	**metal**
1963	25 Jan 1963	– 12 Feb 1964	**water**
1975	11 Feb 1975	– 30 Jan 1976	**wood**
1987	29 Jan 1987	– 16 Feb 1988	**fire**
1999	6 Feb 1999	– 4 Feb 2000	**earth**

Rabbit *Wood–Water* (1903, 1963)
Water enhances rabbit's natural sensitive nature. Unfortunately, these rabbits can empathize with others so much that they become unproductive and shy away from harsh reality. All rabbits dislike conflicts, but water rabbits go to extremes to avoid confrontation. A natural passivity combined with a reflective nature can make them victims of remorse and 'If Only' thoughts.

Rabbit *Wood–Wood* (1915, 1975)
Wood is rabbit's natural element, but it is a two-sided symbol. On the one hand, wood rabbits can be content to

the point of placidity. Alternatively, they may be of the more adventurous type. In these cases, wood opens rabbits up to their emotions – which can also make them vulnerable. Double wood rabbits tend to be easy-going, generous people. They should beware of others trying to take advantage of them. Wood releases the creative powers of rabbit people and enhances their aesthetic taste; therefore these people are artistic and creative.

Rabbit *Wood–Fire* (1927, 1987)
Wood and fire is a curious, flammable mixture that can make rabbit warm and friendly, or moody and bad-tempered. Rabbits are naturally Yin and fire is Yang. One balances the other, so fire can help rabbits use their skills to reach the top. It also helps them to be more expressive. Fire rabbits are more likely to become leaders as they have many admirers and inspire confidence. They should try to follow their true rabbit natures and let reason control passion.

Rabbit *Wood–Earth* (1939, 1999)
Earth endows this rabbit with a more realistic and pragmatic character. Earth rabbits are more able to deal with the downside of life than other rabbits, who typically try to hide from it. Better equipped to make decisions, the earth rabbit will do so carefully and after great deliberation. They tend to be humble and aware of their limitations. Independent and fond of solitude, earth rabbits can achieve much through hard work.

Rabbit *Wood–Metal* (1951, 2011)
Metal gives the naturally timid rabbit greater courage.
Rabbits born in metal years will be forthright and self-
confident, and some say even visionary. They are more
ambitious and can be ruthless underneath their charming
exteriors. Metal rabbits tend to be polite but cold and they
can be indifferent to the feelings of others. For these
reasons, they are often loners. Metal lends strength to a
character but can also make it rigid. It can make rabbit's
naturally conservative nature inflexible to the point of
being reactionary.

 ## RABBIT AND THE ZODIAC OF WESTERN ASTROLOGY

To work out your zodiac sign see p. 26–27.
General character traits of rabbits of the 12 zodiac signs
are given below. Bear in mind that the Western zodiac sign
modifies the basic rabbit nature – especially in the area of
personal relationships.

Aries rabbit Aries brings courage to rabbit, who adds
grace to the equation. Aries rabbits are emotionally both
expressive and vulnerable. Unlike other rabbits, however,
they don't mind taking risks. Success is important to Aries
rabbits.

Taurus rabbit Both Taureans and rabbits are peace-loving,
calm, stay-at-home people; Taurus rabbits doubly so. Their
liking for the good things in life can make them
materialistic, and they should be wary of ostentatious
behaviour.

Gemini rabbit Mercurial Gemini and steady rabbit make an odd mixture. On the surface, a Gemini rabbit seems to be a superficial, turbulent kind of person; in fact, they are constantly on the watch and very analytical. These rabbits are persuasive and like to appear sophisticated and cultured.

Cancer rabbit The close similarities between these two signs can accentuate certain facets of rabbit's nature. Cancer rabbits are doubly cautious, and can be weak. On the whole, they are nice, hospitable people who make good friends.

Leo rabbit At times deceptively calm, Leo rabbits are potentially great achievers. Open in expressing their desires, flamboyant and popular, these people find it hard to be self-restrained or objective. A tendency to be self-centred and pompous is offset by mild manners and a generous nature.

Virgo rabbit Analytical Virgo and careful rabbit combine to make a tendency to worry. These attributes can be used for benefit though, and many Virgo rabbits are wise, considerate types. If their nervous energy is left unused they can be fidgety.

Libra rabbit Sweet-talking and melancholic, these rabbits may appear slightly effeminate. They have very inquiring minds and make good scholars or communicators. Libra rabbits like to surround themselves with the best of everything and can be extravagant; but they work hard to get what they want. A tendency to be snobbish should be watched.

Scorpio rabbit Scorpio rabbits are earnest people – they take themselves very seriously. Scorpio brings great willpower to the rabbit. They are secretive about intimate matters, but not dispassionate. In private, they can be passionate and have a high sex drive; but if they feel insecure, Scorpio rabbits can become deceitful and pedantic.

Sagittarius rabbit This combination makes for the most balanced and easy-going rabbit. Unusually interested in the more exotic side of life, these rabbits are exceptional in that they like to experience adventure. They are not as diplomatic or tactful as other rabbits but are loyal and loving people.

Capricorn rabbit Capricorn rabbits seem to be insensitive due to their brusque natures; underneath, however, they are kind and considerate, supportive and protective towards their family and loved ones. Physically graceful, these rabbits are surprisingly impractical.

Aquarius rabbit Thirsty for knowledge and eager for new experiences, these rabbits are true intellectuals – they often make good writers. Not so much in need of stability and security, Aquarian rabbits like to keep their distance.

Pisces rabbit The most difficult of all rabbits to read; spiritual and perceptive, Pisces deepens rabbit's inherently mysterious nature – such people can even be psychic. Accomplished in the arts, refined and companionable, Pisces rabbits have the ability to live happy, well-ordered lives. Their insecurities can make them appear stubborn at times.

Some famous people born in the years of the rabbit and their zodiac signs

- **Adam Smith**
  Economist
  5 Jun 1723 Gemini

- **Queen Victoria**
  Monarch
  24 May 1819 Gemini

- **Arturo Toscanini**
  Conductor
  25 Mar 1867 Aries

- **Marie Curie**
  Chemist
  7 Nov 1867 Scorpio

- **Albert Einstein**
  Physicist
  14 Mar 1879 Pisces

- **Joseph Stalin**
  Political leader
  21 Dec 1879 Sagittarius

- **Henry Miller**
  Novelist
  26 Dec 1891 Capricorn

- **Benjamin Spock**
  Paediatrician
  2 May 1903 Taurus

- **Bob Hope**
  Comedian/Actor
  29 May 1903 Gemini

- **George Orwell**
  Writer
  25 Jun 1903 Cancer

- **Cary Grant**
  Actor
  18 Jan 1904 Capricorn

- **Orson Welles**
  Actor/Director
  6 May 1915 Taurus

- **Ingrid Bergman**
  Actress
  29 Aug 1915 Virgo

- **Arthur Miller**
  Dramatist
  17 Oct 1915 Libra

- **Frank Sinatra**
  Singer
  12 Dec 1915 Sagittarius

- **Ken Russell**
  Film director
  3 Jul 1927 Cancer

- **Neil Simon**
  Playwright
  4 Jul 1927 Cancer

- **Fidel Castro**
  Political leader
  13 Aug 1927 Leo

- **David Frost**
  TV personality
  7 Apr 1939 Aries

- **James Galway**
  Flautist
  8 Dec 1939 Sagittarius

5. The Dragon
The Yang wood animal

Lunar years ruled by the dragon

1904	16 Feb 1904	–	3 Feb 1905
1916	3 Feb 1916	–	22 Jan 1917
1928	23 Jan 1928	–	9 Feb 1929
1940	8 Feb 1940	–	26 Jan 1941
1952	27 Jan 1952	–	13 Feb 1953
1964	13 Feb 1964	–	1 Feb 1965
1976	31 Jan 1976	–	17 Feb 1977
1988	17 Feb 1988	–	5 Feb 1989
2000	5 Feb 2000	–	23 Jan 2001

The dragon is the only mythical animal in the Chinese zodiac. In China, dragons are associated with strength, health, harmony and good luck; they are placed above doors or on the tops of roofs to banish demons and evil spirits.

THE DRAGON PERSONALITY

Dragons have magnetic, persuasive personalities and are capable of great success or spectacular failure. Normally, however, whatever they set their hearts on doing, they do well; the secret is their great faith in themselves. On the negative side, dragons are renowned for not finishing what they start. The frank and open way in which they approach people and situations can be disconcerting; but their innate sincerity and enthusiasm make up for this.

CHARACTERISTICS

These are the general personality traits of those people who are typical dragons, both at their best and at their worst.

Positive	Negative
● visionary	● demanding
● dynamic	● impatient
● idealistic	● intolerant
● perfectionist	● gullible
● scrupulous	● dissatisfied
● lucky	● overpowering
● successful	● irritable
● enthusiastic	● abrupt
● sentimental	● naive
● healthy	● overzealous
● voluble	● eccentric
● irresistible	● proud
● exciting	● tactless
● intelligent	● short-tempered

SECRET DRAGON

Despite their impressive appearance, deep down dragons are dissatisfied and discontent. The dragon's tireless search for excitement is not always fruitful. They need to be embarking on some new project, campaign or love affair to feel truly alive. Inevitably, depression caused by the unavoidable daily routine will get most dragons down at some time.

ELEMENT

Dragon is linked to the ancient Chinese element of wood. Wood is an ambivalent element. As a crutch it lends support; as a spear it can be used as a weapon. Consequently, dragons are full of both positive and negative energies that will surface in, for example, strong emotions. For instance, emotionally, wood is associated with both anger and kindness.

BALANCE

Dragons spend a lot of time racing from one experience to another. Always set on the latest goal, they are blinkered to failure and try to forget any that occur. Only successes are considered significant. Dragons seem impressive only because they believe that they are, and this amazing self-confidence makes others believe in them also. You could say that the dragon's image is simply a confidence trick. According to Chinese tradition, dragons must confront their image and recognize its illusory nature. Dragons will only be truly content when they accept their vulnerability, and use it to balance their exuberance.

BEST ASSOCIATIONS

Traditionally, the following are said to be associated with dragons:

Taste	acid
Season	spring
Birth	anytime, except during a storm
Colours	yellow, black
Plants	mandrake, sage
Flowers	lotus
Food	wheat, poultry
Climate	windy

THE MALE DRAGON

If a man has a typical dragon personality, he will generally display the behaviour listed below.

- is a natural showman
- is seductively attractive
- will have many admirers
- has a few close friends
- believes he is irreplaceable
- is good at sports
- does not believe he can make mistakes
- is sentimental and passionate about loved ones
- can be impulsive but not a daredevil
- will harbour a grudge for years
- is good-humoured
- enjoys shopping
- has many hobbies and interests

THE FEMALE DRAGON

If a woman has a typical dragon personality, she will generally display the behaviour listed below.

- will not be happy as a housewife
- is generous with both time and money
- can instill confidence in others
- desires perfection in herself and others
- is always attractive, even if not beautiful
- takes revenge on enemies, even if it takes years
- craves attention
- likes to be flattered
- hates to be manipulated or deceived
- tells good jokes
- likes children
- is very straightforward
- needs to feel irreplaceable

THE DRAGON CHILD

If a child has a typical dragon personality, he or she will generally display the behaviour listed below.

- is prone to boredom
- dislikes authority
- needs motivating but potentially a good student
- dislikes demonstrations of affection
- is insolent with teachers
- enjoys, and is good at, sports
- is undemanding as far as attention is concerned
- dislikes timetables
- is inventive
- needs to be given ample freedom to blossom
- has a short attention span
- is gifted but difficult
- feels he or she is misunderstood – often correctly

DRAGON AT HOME

Dragon people suffer from mild claustrophobia – they need space, fresh air and freedom. To live in one place for long is a chore for a dragon. If they have settled down, dragons like to live in ultra-modern houses, on board a houseboat or near the coast where they can hear the thunder of the ocean. If such options are not available, a dragon will at least try to redecorate frequently to keep boredom at bay. However pleasant their home environment though, dragons will spend more time out and about than sitting at home.

DRAGON AT WORK

Dragons are not power-hungry people, but they tend to end up at the top of their profession, simply because this is what they do best – lead. They are terrible at carrying out mundane tasks but excel at solving problems that others have found insoluble. They make great directors and troubleshooters. Dragons inspire confidence in others and are good promoters or sellers; their integrity lends credibility to whatever they do. Dragons need to feel vital at work and be in a position that allows them to innovate or create.

Some typical dragon occupations

- managing director
- salesperson
- advertising executive
- president or prime minister
- prophet
- barrister
- film producer
- photojournalist
- architect
- professional speaker
- philosopher
- astronaut
- artist
- film star
- war correspondent

DRAGON PREFERENCES

Likes

- any sort of celebration such as parties and festivals
- to wear casual, comfortable clothes
- going on holiday and travelling
- to be taken seriously
- picnics
- fun fairs, especially the roller coaster
- watching fireworks
- being asked for help
- giving advice
- to feel irreplaceable
- to be in charge
- championing causes

Dislikes

- having to be calm and patient
- waiting for anything or anyone
- a lack of vision in others
- having nothing to do
- manipulative people
- listening to advice
- dishonesty and hypocrisy
- lack of energy or willpower in others
- being patronized
- compromise

GOOD FRIENDS FOR DRAGONS

The diagram below shows the compatibility of dragon with other animals. There is no fixed ruling, however, because there are other influences on both the dragon and any potential friend. These influences are:

- the companion in life (see pp. 23–25)
- the dominant element (from the year of birth)

Compatibility of dragon with other animals

▲ Rat	○ Dragon	▲ Monkey
▼ Ox	▲ Snake	■ Rooster
▲ Tiger	■ Horse	▼ Dog
○ Rabbit	○ Goat	● Pig

Key

▲ Highly compatible
● Amicable
■ No conflict but needs some effort
○ Lack of sympathy
▼ Antagonistic

Rat with dragon Both are easily bored, so plenty of activity can be expected, although rat may have to let dragon take the dominant role. Dragons love admiration, so a relationship could work.

Ox with dragon Any relationship between these two will not be long-lived. Ox enjoys daily routine; dragon is always trying to escape from it. If they can compromise, both could gain something positive from the experience.

Tiger with dragon These two are very similar in temperament and both are energetic and courageous. Any relationship between them will never be boring but could become a struggle for dominance.

Rabbit with dragon Unlikely to get on, dragons annoy rabbits with their madcap, untidy natures. A compromise could be achieved if both have their own space. Rabbits can teach dragons tact.

Dragon with dragon Two dragons make a glittering partnership, although each of them may actually be more in love with themselves as a couple than with their partner as an individual. But dragons have to feel needed, and this cannot be satisfied by another equally demanding dragon.

Snake with dragon A well-matched couple, snakes are clever enough to let dragons think they are in charge. Dragons are pleased to associate with elegant snakes. Together, they can achieve a lot.

Horse with dragon Enthusiastic horse and energetic dragon can get on well together if they share a common purpose and dragon does not invade horse's privacy too much. Self-preoccupied horses are not able to give dragons the attention they crave.

Goat with dragon Lack of understanding can blight any relationship between these two, unless both learn to accept and appreciate their differences. Business alliances will be more successful than personal ones as dragons can help quiet goats realize their creativity.

Monkey with dragon Dragons are attracted to monkeys' charm and intelligence. The two inspire and complement each another without becoming rivals – they will have many friends and a busy social life.

Rooster with dragon Both these characters can be found in the limelight: roosters for reassurance; dragons as it is their natural habitat. This can bolster both their egos, but misunderstandings will occur.

Dog with dragon The intellectual but cynical dog will deflate a dragon's self-confidence. Dogs are able to see the dragon's image for the mirage it is – they are unable to admire a dragon.

Pig with dragon Pigs and dragons have little in common, but the two can be very compatible. Pig is easy-going and will enjoy dragon's showy nature. Dragon will sweep pig off his feet, and pig will adore and fuss over the dragon.

DRAGON IN LOVE

Dragons are never short of admirers and never suffer from unrequited love. They are passionate but never blinded by this. Dragons are very self-reliant and know that they could live without their partner. Although they are often loved, dragons fall in love rarely. Once in love, dragons are very loyal and loving. In fact, their partners are put on pedestals. If a dragon discovers that his or her partner is unworthy of their devotion, the dragon will be hurt and soon end the relationship. Otherwise, it is difficult to break a dragon's heart because first you have to damage their invulnerable egos.

DRAGON AND SEX

Sex is very important for dragons. They often embark on amorous adventures at an early age, and see sexual expression as the key to their personal freedom. This is not necessarily a good thing for dragon bed-partners because dragons have a tendency to view their lovers as instruments to bring about their great escape and not as individuals. Nevertheless, whatever dragons do, they perform well. They are not selfish or unimaginative lovers, just a bit impersonal maybe. Dragons in love will lavish affection on their partner and will do anything to please them.

HEALTH

Dragon's element, wood, is associated with the liver, so dragons should pay particular attention to keeping this organ in working order. Despite being associated with health and vitality, dragons often suffer from insomnia and respiratory problems. All dragons, however, take care of themselves to their best ability so they rarely get very sick. If they do, dragons normally recover quickly. When feeling vulnerable, dragons have a tendency to overeat and should watch out for this.

LEISURE INTERESTS

Dragons have many interests but often lack the staying power to learn the necessary skills. A typical dragon will be enthusiastically learning yoga one week, judo the next and the saxophone for a while as well. Anything exciting, bold or adventurous appeals. It cannot be something that involves too much training, but dragons will be keen to go on short breaks, where tuition or guidance is provided – a skiing holiday or safari, for example – and where they can still feel daring without taking many risks, as long as they can master the skills quickly and not spend too much time on the nursery slopes. Otherwise, they love to go backpacking somewhere like the Himalayas, where they feel at home in the lofty peaks.

THE DRAGON YEARS AND THEIR ELEMENTS

The dragon is a Yang wood animal. Each of the dragon years, however, is associated with an element which is said to have its own influence. These elements are wood, fire, earth, metal and water. They influence dragon in a regular sequence, which is repeated every 60 years. In the table opposite, for example, the dragon year 1904 is a wood year. The next dragon wood year is 60 years later in 1964, and the next will be 2024. Dragon's natural element is wood; the influence of this combines with those of the element of the year of birth. The possible effects of the year elements are listed opposite.

	Lunar years ruled by the dragon and their elements	
1904	16 Feb 1904 – 3 Feb 1905	**wood**
1916	3 Feb 1916 – 22 Jan 1917	**fire**
1928	23 Jan 1928 – 9 Feb 1929	**earth**
1940	8 Feb 1940 – 26 Jan 1941	**metal**
1952	27 Jan 1952 – 13 Feb 1953	**water**
1964	13 Feb 1964 – 1 Feb 1965	**wood**
1976	31 Jan 1976 – 17 Feb 1977	**fire**
1988	17 Feb 1988 – 5 Feb 1989	**earth**
2000	5 Feb 2000 – 23 Jan 2001	**metal**

Dragon *Wood–Wood* (1904, 1964)

Wood dragons are in their natural element. Wood, a symbol of growth and renewal, allows dragon to be a creative, innovative person fond of improvisation. They love harmony, elegance and all beautiful things. Relaxed and at ease socially, these dragons do not like to offend people. Wood can bring pessimism to a character, but dragons temper this tendency with their dynamism. They are progressive people, and untypically curious of affairs not centred around them. Dramatic and generous, wood dragons are fun and considerate people.

Dragon *Wood–Fire* (1916, 1976)

Potentially a highly combustible combination of fire and wood, fire dragons are actually warm-hearted and honest. They are temperamental and have no patience at all. Ambitious and proud, fire dragons tend to be authoritarian. They are perfectionists and will be highly critical if someone does not have the same standards or even opinions as them. All dragons are charismatic, fire dragons are inspirational – many are famous or infamous people.

Dragon *Wood–Earth* (1928, 1988)
Like all dragons, earth dragons like to dedicate themselves to a cause or project. Earth allows dragons to be more cooperative and open to team work than typical dragons, who are just as likely to embark on a solitary quest. Earth dragons don't mind paying attention to the details of a plan. Earth brings patience to the dragon, so they are not in such a hurry. Stability and security are important to these dragons, who will probably equate them with financial independence.

Dragon *Wood–Metal* (1940, 2000)
Metal strengthens many of dragon's qualities. Metal dragons are very theatrical and have enormous egos. Already resolute, they are argumentative to the point of aggression, but always honest. If a metal dragon believes in a cause, he or she will single-mindedly champion it against all odds. Bordering on the heroic, these dragons have the natures of gladiators. Visionary but still practical, efficient and hard-working, metal dragons are often successful.

Dragon *Wood–Water* (1952, 2012)
Normally, water would make a character calm and reflective. On dragons, however, the opposite can be true unless the dragon learns to balance the water tendency with his innate dragon excessiveness. Nevertheless, water dragons are more diplomatic than average dragons and

very creative. They are pacifists and interested in social problems. This, combined with their intuitive wisdom, makes water dragons idealistic and compassionate.

DRAGON AND THE ZODIAC OF WESTERN ASTROLOGY

To work out your zodiac sign see p. 26–27. General character traits of dragons of the 12 zodiac signs are given below. Bear in mind that the Western zodiac sign modifies the basic dragon nature – especially in the area of personal relationships.

Aries dragon Two energetic signs make Aries dragons almost hyperactive. Their enthusiasm is infectious, but they need to learn to finish what they start. Selfish and impulsive, these dragons lead turbulent lives and tend to be excessively arrogant.

Taurus dragon Taurean dragons are more down-to-earth than typical dragons while still being outward-looking and creative. They have great staying power and are more likely to finish a project and achieve fame easily. Taurus dragons are sentimental and sensuous people.

Gemini dragon Airy Gemini and enthusiastic dragon combine to make a real character. These people have a razor-sharp wit and are verbally adroit. Gemini dragons are not fools; they use humour to make a serious point and are very principled.

Cancer dragon Cancer dragons are profound in their thoughts and feelings, but they can be too sensitive. Cancer tones down some of the dragon's qualities, making them less brash and reckless and more cautious. These dragons are very good at rousing and inspiring others to achieve their aims.

Leo dragon Leo dragons are exhausting, excessive and superior – with good reason though. They are, however, noble at heart and basically good-humoured. Leo dragons love to bestow their generosity on others less fortunate than themselves. They are hospitable but need to be the centre of everyone's attention.

Virgo dragon Analytical Virgo and brash dragon do not always make a harmonious combination. They are precise, cannot resist an intellectual challenge, and love solving puzzles. As dragons, these people are not so 'make-believe'; they are more realistic. Underneath their harsh exteriors, however, they are well-meaning people.

Libra dragon Manipulative Libra allows dragon to be a more reassuring person, but deceptively so. Unusually diplomatic, they find it easy to rally support and take the lead. Libra dragons are refined and intelligent; style, taste and quality are important to them.

Scorpio dragon Passionate and unpredictable, Scorpio dragons often provoke strong reactions and create intense dramas. They never compromise or give up. Dragons are suspicious anyway, but combined with Scorpio's jealous and vengeful nature this is not a person to have as an enemy.

Sagittarius dragon Friendly and relatively quiet, Sagittarius dragons are fun-loving optimists. They are proud of their ability to get on with anyone and unlike most dragons they do not suffer from arrogance. Expressive but not sentimental, Sagittarius dragon is not afraid to take great risks.

Capricorn dragon Although eloquent about worldly matters, Capricornean dragons find it difficult to express their personal feelings. At times they seem hard and ambitious, but underneath they are really compassionate and sensitive.

Aquarius dragon Aquarius allows the dragon to be calm and lucid and even capable of self-criticism – unique among dragons. They have inquisitive and versatile minds but find it difficult to relax. Despite being popular and sociable people, at heart Aquarian dragons are pessimists.

Pisces dragon Watery Pisces dampens many of the dragon's fiery qualities. Pisces dragons are wise and inspired but they are also enigmatic, making it hard to understand their motives. Often, they appear to have their head in the clouds but are in fact very shrewd people. On the whole, these dragons are loving and charming but they will be defensive and demanding if insecure.

Some famous people born in the years of the dragon and their zodiac signs

- **Charles Darwin**
  Naturalist
  12 Feb 1809 Aquarius

- **Florence Nightingale**
  Nurse
  12 May 1820 Taurus

- **Friedrich Nietzsche**
  Philosopher
  15 Oct 1844 Libra

- **Sigmund Freud**
  Neurologist
  6 May 1856 Taurus

- **George Bernard Shaw**
  Playwright
  26 Jul 1856 Leo

- **Bing Crosby**
  Singer
  2 May 1904 Taurus

- **Salvador Dali**
  Painter
  11 May 1904 Taurus

- **Graham Greene**
  Writer
  2 Oct 1904 Libra

- **Gregory Peck**
  Actor
  5 Apr 1916 Aries

- **Yehudi Menuhin**
  Violinist
  22 Apr 1916 Taurus

- **Kirk Douglas**
  Actor
  9 Dec 1916 Sagittarius

- **Eartha Kitt**
  Singer
  26 Jan 1928 Aquarius

- **Shirley Temple**
  Actress
  23 Apr 1928 Taurus

- **Che Guevara**
  Revolutionary
  14 Jun 1928 Gemini

- **Stanley Kubrick**
  Filmmaker
  26 Jul 1928 Leo

- **Martin Luther King**
  Civil rights leader
  15 Jan 1929 Capricorn

- **John Lennon**
  Singer/Composer
  9 Oct 1940 Libra

- **Cliff Richard**
  Singer
  14 Oct 1940 Libra

- **Pelé**
  Footballer
  23 Oct 1940 Scorpio

- **Pierce Brosnan**
  Actor
  16 May 1952 Taurus

6. The Snake
The Yin fire animal

Lunar years ruled by the snake				
1905	4 Feb 1905	–	24 Jan 1906
1917	23 Jan 1917	–	10 Feb 1918
1929	10 Feb 1929	–	29 Jan 1930
1941	27 Jan 1941	–	14 Feb 1942
1953	14 Feb 1953	–	2 Feb 1954
1965	2 Feb 1965	–	20 Jan 1966
1977	18 Feb 1977	–	6 Feb 1978
1989	6 Feb 1989	–	26 Jan 1990
2001	24 Jan 2001	–	11 Feb 2002

There are few animals with more symbolic associations than the snake. Chinese mythology holds that a half-human snake was the father of the Chinese emperors.

THE SNAKE PERSONALITY

In the West, the snake is often seen as evil. The snake of Chinese astrology, however, is associated with beauty and wisdom. Snakes may appear languid and serene, but they are always mentally active. Snakes are deep thinkers and give very good advice – but they cannot take it. Snakes are capable of lying to get out of a scrape. Linked with esoteric knowledge and spiritual discovery, snakes are sacred to many peoples. Snakes are often people who are, or are interested in, the psychic, the mystical or the religious.

CHARACTERISTICS

These are the general personality traits of those people who are typical snakes, both at their best and at their worst.

Positive	Negative
● distinguished	● extravagant
● elegant	● vengeful
● self-contained	● obstinate
● shrewd	● calculating
● profound	● mean with money
● perceptive	● cruel
● lucid	● self-doubting
● sophisticated	● suspicious
● wise	● crafty
● gregarious	● remote
● sensual	● possessive
● curious	● anxious
● reflective	● jealous
● organized	● dishonest

SECRET **SNAKE**
The typical image of a snake is one basking in the sun
doing nothing. Many interpret this as laziness. In fact,
snakes are very hard-working. If something needs to
be done, snake will not shy away from it. The secret is
their efficiency. Snakes will get the job done in the
quickest, most economical way, which is why they
always have plenty of time to relax.

ELEMENT
Snake is linked to the ancient Chinese element of fire.
Fire is a dynamic, exciting sign, which is balanced by
snake's innate Yin tendency. The energy of fire can be
expressed positively and negatively. It brings warmth,
comfort and light, and it protects. But fire can also
burn and destroy. For example, emotionally fire is
associated with cruelty and intolerance as well as love
and respect. Fire people are always attractive.

BALANCE
Snakes and dragons are especially karmic signs. Put
simply, karma is a person's destiny. Each action
performed affects the next and so on, into infinity.
The Chinese believe that snakes particularly must deal
with their karmic problems within their lifetime to
achieve balance. This should not be too much of a
problem as snakes are generally well-balanced people.
Their natural wisdom grants them the ability to deal
with life gracefully and they are usually unperturbed
by life's ups and downs. Tendencies to watch are their
highly individual approach to morality and honesty –
that is, snakes do or say whatever is most convenient
for them.

BEST ASSOCIATIONS

Traditionally, the following are said to be associated with snakes:

● **Taste**	bitter
● **Season**	summer
● **Birth**	warm, summer day
● **Colours**	green, red
● **Plant**	ferns
● **Flower**	heather, thistle
● **Food**	rice, lamb
● **Climate**	hot, sunny

THE MALE SNAKE

If a man has a typical snake personality, he will generally display the behaviour listed below.

- is a bad loser
- does not tolerate insults
- is influential
- does not understand fidelity
- will be handsome and well groomed
- is a hedonist
- may be a snob at times
- is romantic and passionate
- has a subtle sense of humour
- relies on first impressions
- is an unlucky gambler

THE FEMALE SNAKE

If a woman has a typical snake personality, she will generally display the behaviour listed below.

- is witty and humorous
- takes failure personally
- gives good advice
- will be captivatingly beautiful
- is not prone to false modesty
- likes her home comforts
- is eager to please others
- will exact her revenge on enemies
- is more faithful than male snakes
- is uncannily perceptive

THE SNAKE CHILD

If a child has a typical snake personality, he or she will generally display the behaviour listed below.

- is tranquil and problem-free
- is basically happy
- needs to learn how to share toys
- is sensitive to family quarrels
- is good at arts subjects at school
- performs erratically at school
- is calm – if family is settled
- seeks to please parents
- likes secrets and confidences
- does not mind responsibility
- is jealous of parents' attentions
- demands a lot of affection

SNAKE AT HOME

Home is snake's favourite place. They will try to create a calm and peaceful environment but in an imaginative way. Snakes can naturally combine colours and designs in a tasteful way. Furnishings are chosen to indulge the snake's sensuous nature – they will be sumptuously comfortable. The larder will always be well stocked with the finest foods and drinks, and there will be plenty of books to read. A snake home is likely to have expensive items such as antiques and works of art on display. If so, they will not be fakes. In some way, snakes' homes will reflect their perception of themselves. For example, snakes will make their surroundings elegant, witty or austere depending on their personalities. Snakes' need to stamp their personality on their homes makes them difficult people to live with.

SNAKE AT WORK

Snakes are very efficient and adaptable people. They will do something quickly with the minimum of fuss and in the most cost-effective way. They are also quite capable of quietly eliminating the competition. Although they are wilful and well organized, snakes are not so good at long-term planning. A snake is more likely to rely on chance and wits. This does not mean, however, that they take risks. Snakes are opportunistic and ambitious but combine this with deliberation not recklessness. Wisdom allows snakes to be objective about their goals and aspirations. Snakes can be very determined and persevering if they are morally or materially inspired. If they are not motivated or have nothing to do, they will revert to their natural reflective pose – which others may interpret as laziness.

Some typical snake occupations

- professor
- linguist
- philosopher
- teacher
- psychiatrist
- ambassador
- anything related to the arcane
- astrologer
- clairvoyant
- personnel officer
- public relations executive
- mediator
- interior designer

SNAKE PREFERENCES

Likes

- to please others
- ornaments
- dressing to impress
- confiding and hearing confessions
- deserts and wild landscapes
- to impress others with their knowledge
- to make gestures of good will
- a good debate
- to spend extravagantly on themselves
- abstract art
- applause
- harmony and stability
- to be asked for help

Dislikes

- people getting out of control
- to be found gullible
- prejudiced people
- to be made an example of
- disputes and violence
- to lend or give others money
- superficial people
- vulgarity
- to be abandoned
- fake anything

GOOD FRIENDS FOR SNAKES

The diagram below shows the compatibility of snake with other animals. There is no fixed ruling, however, because there are other influences on both the snake and any potential friend. These influences are:

- the companion in life (see pp. 23–25)
- the dominant element (from the year of birth)

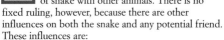

Compatibility of snake with other animals		
● Rat	▲ Dragon	▼ Monkey
● Ox	■ Snake	▲ Rooster
○ Tiger	○ Horse	■ Dog
▲ Rabbit	● Goat	▼ Pig

Key

▲ Highly compatible
● Amicable
■ No conflict but needs some effort
○ Lack of sympathy
▼ Antagonistic

Rat with snake This is a friendly pair who both enjoy fine things and will gossip together for hours. Snake can blow hot and cold and may be possessive one moment and wander off to new pastures the next, but all this will be temporary.

Ox with snake Oxen are dependable and will give snakes the support they need. Both like to work towards long-term goals and ox can help snake do this effectively. Each will respect the other's need for privacy and all should go well as long as the snakes do not reveal their manipulative sides.

Tiger with snake Snake and tiger approach life from opposite angles. Snakes follow their heads and tigers follow their hearts; snakes enjoy relaxing with a book while tigers like action and risk. Both would misunderstand, and feel suspicious of, the other's motivations.

Rabbit with snake This can be a good match. Both snakes and rabbits cultivate peace and security and share a love of the arts. Snake can help rabbit be more adventurous, as long as rabbit is tolerant of snake's less virtuous nature.

Dragon with snake A well-matched couple, snakes are clever enough to let dragons think they are in charge. Dragons are pleased to be with elegant, seductive snakes. Together, they can achieve a lot.

Snake with snake A good combination for work and friendship, but not for a long-term relationship. In business, they will be ruthless and ambitious. For two snakes to live together, one would eventually be smothered by the other and no snake likes to be dominated.

Horse with snake At first, there will be a mutual attraction of opposites between the out-going horse and the more reticent snake. The horse will soon tire of thoughtful snake who, in turn, will tire of horse's lack of mental concentration.

Goat with snake Both the goat and the snake love art, beauty and harmony. The snake appreciates goat's imagination and creativity. As long as life is good, these two will rarely argue as it is too much trouble. Otherwise, the goat may find snake too serious and snake will think goat weak.

Monkey with snake The monkey is intelligent in a quick-witted sort of way, the snake in a more profound fashion. This can lead to competition or a perfect business relationship. In love, however, the monkey finds snake boring and will not settle down.

Rooster with snake This is the most ideal couple of Chinese astrology. They balance each other like mind and matter. Snake and rooster both flatter and understand the other.

Dog with snake Idealistic dog is attracted to snake's wisdom and depth and will ignore the snake's selfish, ambitious streak. Snakes admire the dog's honesty and, as long as snakes do not mind being idealized, this relationship could work out.

Pig with snake This is a case of opposites that do not attract. Snake sees the pig as naive and innocent but the pig is wise to snake's true nature. Both are very sensual creatures and this can unite them. If a relationship does endure, it is likely to be thanks to the pig's giving nature.

SNAKE IN LOVE

Snakes are intense and passionate people. They have to feel they are the centre of their lover's life. Often, this will smother a relationship. Snakes, however, will not curb their naturally flirtatious habits – they like to check that their sex appeal is still operational. Before they settle down, snakes will have many love affairs, liaisons and intrigues; this may not stop once they are married. Snakes expect fidelity but may not be faithful themselves. Partners of snake people should try and remain a little independent to gain the snake's respect. Snakes will not like this but will admire them for it and will try harder to be faithful.

SNAKE AND SEX

Witty, passionate and sensual, snakes are exciting and imaginative lovers. Like dragons, snakes use sex as a means of self-discovery. They will blossom in a relationship that is physically compatible. Snakes enjoy being intimate both physically and emotionally but they are not as faithful as the dragon. Highly seductive, they enchant others by being almost hypnotically attentive to them and they cannot abide to be resisted. Snakes do not undertake a seduction lightly – so do not toy with snake people's affections or they may show you their more dangerous, vengeful side.

HEALTH

Snake's element, fire, is associated with the heart and the small intestine, so snakes should pay particular attention to keeping these organs in working order. They should have regular medical check-ups for their heart. Stomach aches are a common snake complaint, so try to cut down on rich, indigestible foods. Snakes need to learn to control their passions and indulgent natures. Sensitive and highly strung, snakes have a tendency for nervous disorders.

LEISURE INTERESTS

Snakes like nothing better than to curl up with a good book in their favourite chair with some classical music in the background. Relaxing in the country at the weekend is another favourite snake pastime. When they go out, snakes like to frequent the theatre and love opera. These pursuits allow them to indulge their love of dressing up as well as their enjoyment of the 'finer' things in life. Snakes are great strategists, and they excel at games like backgammon and chess. At home, if they are not relaxing, snakes will undertake home improvements such as painting and decorating or just rearranging the ornaments.

THE SNAKE YEARS AND THEIR ELEMENTS

The snake is a Yin fire animal. Each of the snake years, however, is associated with an element which is said to have its own influence. These elements are wood, fire, earth, metal and water. They influence snake in a regular sequence, which is repeated every 60 years. In the table below, for example, the snake year 1905 is a wood year. The next snake wood year is 60 years later in 1965, and the next will be 2025. Snake's natural element is fire; the influence of this combines with those of the element of the year of birth. The possible effects of the year elements are listed below.

Lunar years ruled by the snake and their elements			
1905	4 Feb 1905	– 24 Jan 1906	wood
1917	23 Jan 1917	– 10 Feb 1918	fire
1929	10 Feb 1929	– 29 Jan 1930	earth
1941	27 Jan 1941	– 14 Feb 1942	metal
1953	14 Feb 1953	– 2 Feb 1954	water
1965	2 Feb 1965	– 20 Jan 1966	wood
1977	18 Feb 1977	– 6 Feb 1978	fire
1989	6 Feb 1989	– 26 Jan 1990	earth
2001	24 Jan 2001	– 11 Feb 2002	metal

Snake *Fire–Wood* (1905, 1965)
Fire and wood can sometimes be a flammable combination. Normally, however, wood snakes are laid-back, easy-going and not as ruthless or vindictive as other snakes. Unusual for snakes, they can even be sympathetic and will work for the benefit of others, not just themselves. Wood is a creative element and allows the snake's imagination to run free. Wood snakes are often inventive or creative people who work to combine beauty of form with space. Many are poets, painters or musicians.

Snake *Fire–Fire* (1917, 1977)
Snakes born in fire years are in their natural element. Double fire means double Yang, so they are very dynamic,

almost unstoppable people of action. Fire inflames the energies but can be destructive. They are passionate in the intensity of their feelings towards both their lovers and their enemies. In other animal signs, fire can be destructive, but snakes are Yin and therefore have the wisdom to control their excesses and use their energies positively. Like all fiery people, fire snakes are dramatic, appealing and very sexy. These snakes are not as profound as other snakes.

Snake *Fire–Earth* (1929, 1989)
Earth is a very good element for the snake. They undergo a deep transformation that allows a ripening of many of the snake's qualities. Snakes born in earth years are less mysterious and easy to get to know. Friendly and calm, these snakes try to see the best in people and are not so quick to use others for their own ends. Earth snakes prefer harmony to status. They are not as ambitious as other snakes – they will still achieve their goals but these will not be so grand. Earth can make these snakes introverted; they are so busy recalling dreams or remembering the past that they do not look to the future.

Snake *Fire–Metal* (1941, 2001)
Metal brings strength of character to any animal sign. In the snake, this strength wavers between beauty and destruction. Metal snakes are energetic and self-disciplined people, often perfectionists. They have a very strong sense of self and are the most independent of all snakes. Always reflective, metal makes these snakes very serious people; the rigidity of metal can incline them to fanatical thinking though. These

snakes are intolerant, proud and ruthless, but, unlike other snakes, metal ones are always honest.

Snake *Fire–Water* (1953, 2013)

Reflective water combines with mysterious snake to produce one of the most enigmatic of all signs. Both water and snake are intuitive, so this snake can be intuitive to the point of clairvoyance. The Yin of water balances the Yang of fire but water snakes should not let this element douse their inner fires. Snake's natural element, fire, stops these water people being too passive, although the water does express itself as a pacifist streak. A case of still waters run deep, these snakes are calm, wise and reflective. They are more just and honest than other snakes but still practical and intelligent.

 ## SNAKE AND THE ZODIAC OF WESTERN ASTROLOGY

To work out your zodiac sign see p. 26–27. General character traits of snakes of the 12 zodiac signs are given below. Bear in mind that the Western zodiac sign modifies the basic snake nature – especially in the area of personal relationships.

Aries snake Two fire signs, talented Aries and intelligent snake, combine to make a more powerful, pythonesque snake. They are more impulsive and less reserved than other snakes.

Taurus snake Taurus brings industriousness to the snake. Unusually faithful, they are still charming. Do not be fooled by their decadent air though, as snake's wisdom and Taurean practicality keeps them down-to-earth.

Gemini snake Quick-witted Gemini and profound snake combine the two traits in their conversation – dazzling others with eloquence on any sophisticated or intellectual subject. They should beware of being too clever and missing obvious truths.

Cancer snake Cancerians are prone to depression, but snake relieves this trait. These snakes can recognize their own weaknesses and thus avoid indulging them. Although Cancer snakes can be temperamental, they are basically well-meaning.

Leo snake Both fire signs, they combine to make an energetic and well-balanced individual. Noble lion makes this snake more generous and open. Leo snakes are endearing and have a lusty and adventurous approach to life but they can be self-righteous and competitive.

Virgo snake Virgo snakes are both analytical and intuitive. Often theatrical but always sophisticated and stylish, they can appear intimidating or calculating to others. More cautious about romance, Virgo snakes are serious about matters of the heart.

Libra snake Idealistic Libra and wise snake make a magnetic combination. They are polite and great diplomats. Do not be deceived by their placid appearance though. All snakes dislike vulgar outbursts, but if a Libra snake is roused then beware.

Scorpio snake Suspicious Scorpio accentuates the snake's crafty, scheming side. They are always competitive, even at times when it is inappropriate.

This makes their lives unnecessarily complicated. Sagittarius snake Honourable snakes who have a sense of morality that other snakes lack, they feel more social responsibility and are generous with money. They are not as bothered with their appearance as other snakes, which makes them more approachable.

Capricorn snake Resolute Capricorn and ambitious snake make highly materialistic and status-seeking people. They are good providers and like to create a solid family base. They are even more profound than typical snakes but are too reserved. Capricornean snakes should relax a bit.

Aquarius snake Born under two intuitive signs, these snakes are almost too visionary and esoteric. Very individualistic, Aquarian snakes appear eccentric, but they are not bothered by others' opinions and make friends quickly.

Pisces snake On the surface, Piscean snakes are self-composed and appear cool. Underneath, they are kind but not courageous. The snake's great intellect is unfocussed in those born under Pisces; these snakes are dreamers and idealists and are consequently often disillusioned.

Some famous people born in the years of the snake and their zodiac signs

- **Franz Schubert**
  Composer
  31 Jan 1797 Aquarius

- **Edgar Allan Poe**
  Writer
  19 Jan 1809 Capricorn

- **Alfred Lord Tennyson**
  Poet
  6 Aug 1809 Leo

- **Alfred Nobel**
  Inventor
  21 Oct 1833 Libra

- **Mohandas K. Gandhi**
  Political leader
  2 Oct 1869 Libra

- **Henri Matisse**
  Painter
  31 Dec 1869 Capricorn

- **Cecil B. De Mille**
  Filmmaker
  12 Aug 1881 Leo

- **P.G. Wodehouse**
  Writer
  15 Oct 1881 Libra

- **Pablo Picasso**
  Artist
  25 Oct 1881 Scorpio

- **Mao Tse-Tung**
  Political leader
  26 Dec 1893 Capricorn

- **Jean-Paul Sartre**
  Philosopher
  21 Jun 1905 Cancer

- **Greta Garbo**
  Actress
  18 Sep 1905 Virgo

- **John F. Kennedy**
  US President
  29 May 1917 Gemini

- **Robert Mitchum**
  Actor
  6 Aug 1917 Leo

- **Indira Gandhi**
  Stateswoman
  19 Nov 1917 Scorpio

- **André Previn**
  Conductor
  6 Apr 1929 Aries

- **Audrey Hepburn**
  Actress
  4 May 1929 Taurus

- **Jackie Kennedy Onassis**
  First lady
  28 Jul 1929 Leo

- **Grace Kelly**
  Actress
  12 Nov 1929 Scorpio

- **Bob Dylan**
  Singer/Songwriter
  24 May 1941 Gemini

7. The Horse
The Yang fire animal

Lunar years ruled by the horse			
1906	25 Jan 1906	–	12 Feb 1907
1918	11 Feb 1918	–	31 Jan 1919
1930	30 Jan 1930	–	16 Feb 1931
1942	15 Feb 1942	–	4 Feb 1943
1954	3 Feb 1954	–	23 Jan 1955
1966	21 Jan 1966	–	8 Feb 1967
1978	7 Feb 1978	–	27 Jan 1979
1990	27 Jan 1990	–	14 Feb 1991
2002	12 Feb 2002	–	31 Jan 2003

The horse is associated with grace, elegance, bravery and nobility. In China, the horse is the symbol of freedom.

THE HORSE PERSONALITY

Horses approach life with contagious enthusiasm. They are usually happy and will have many friends. They love to chat, converse or orate. Horses have good images – others see in their zest for life bravery and independence – but they are actually quite cowardly. Although they love freedom, horses are not truly independent as they rely on others for support and encouragement that is vital to their wellbeing.

CHARACTERISTICS

These are the general personality traits of those people who are typical horses, at their best and at their worst.

Positive	Negative
● loyal	● unstable
● noble	● temperamental
● cheerful	● impatient
● enthusiastic	● insecure
● enterprising	● hot-tempered
● flexible	● irresponsible
● sincere	● superficial
● frank	● ambitious
● versatile	● careless
● talkative	● spendthrift
● gregarious	● contradictory
● generous	● vain
● unselfish	● easily panicked
● realist	● vulnerable
● energetic	● anxious

SECRET HORSE

On the surface, horses appear to be very self-assured and fearless. Underneath, however, horses are weak and fragile creatures. They are easily scared and let themselves get carried away by their emotions.

ELEMENT

Horse is linked to the ancient Chinese element of fire. Fire is a dynamic, exciting sign, which is enhanced by the horse's innate Yang tendency. The energy of fire can be expressed both positively and negatively. It brings warmth, light and protection as well as the ability to burn and destroy. In horses, fire expresses itself erratically, making them both dynamic and temperamental.

BALANCE

Horses are both fire and Yang. Therefore, they naturally have great reserves of strength. Yet people born under this sign, although seemingly self-confident, are too easily affected by the opinions of others. Criticism or hostility, no matter how slight, shatters their vulnerable egos. Horses will only have access to their full strengths when they have learned to balance their need for approval with faith in themselves.

BEST ASSOCIATIONS

Traditionally, the following are said to be associated with horses:

Taste	bitter
Season	summer
Birth	winter
Colours	orange
Plants	palm tree
Flowers	hawthorn
Food	rice, lamb
Climate	hot, sunny

THE MALE HORSE

If a man has a typical horse personality, he will generally display the behaviour listed below.

- is not very good with money
- is secretly a pessimist
- will always try to look good
- is egocentric
- will offend others without realizing it
- is independent
- needs approval
- likes the sound of his own voice
- appears to be cheerful and easy-going
- is sloppy at home

THE FEMALE HORSE

If a woman has a typical horse personality, she will generally display the behaviour listed below.

- does not like authority
- will never tolerate a subordinate role
- has no time for the problems of others
- craves flattery and attention
- is elegant and well groomed
- is always late
- enjoys dramatic scenes
- needs her own space
- is a good persuader

THE HORSE CHILD

If a child has a typical horse personality, he or she will generally display the behaviour listed below.

- is prone to temper tantrums
- is independent
- has a lazy tendency
- is impetuous
- gives up difficult tasks quickly
- is carefree and lively
- dislikes responsibility
- is untidy and disordered
- prefers playing to learning
- is easy to love
- is difficult to discipline

HORSE AT HOME

Horses are not great home lovers. Often, they prefer to spend time at other people's houses. Nevertheless, a stable home base is actually very important to the horse. They need one to bolster their fragile self-confidence. Horses will appreciate their homes more if they go away occasionally. Horses like to be proud of their home environments, but decorations in the house of a horse are unlikely to be imaginative or original. Also, they are not very good at housework. The home of a horse will be clean but untidy. Horses are not particularly materialistic people. They will decorate their homes with things of sentimental rather than real value.

HORSE AT WORK

Horses tend to be talented people rather than particularly intelligent. They need to have a job with variety to keep them interested and to exploit their versatile natures. Horse people are fast-talking and fast-thinking but are not good at long-term planning or organization. They are not suited to bureaucratic positions as horses hate routine and are unable to pay attention to details. They are skilled communicators, however, and very imaginative. Horses are great to have at brain-storming sessions as they will come up with many ideas – but don't expect them to carry out the ideas. Impatient for results, they are better at initiating projects than performing them. Initially, horses inspire confidence in others as they appear to be supremely confident and enthusiastic about their work. This enthusiasm crumbles at the least mishap, though, and the colleagues of horse will soon lose their faith in these inconstant creatures.

Some typical horse occupations

- athlete
- cowboy
- technician
- administrator
- chauffeur
- inventor
- lorry driver
- sales person
- teacher
- reporter
- painter
- advertising executive
- poet
- hairdresser
- publican
- tour guide

HORSE PREFERENCES

Likes

- beginning a new project
- to be complimented
- dancing
- to make people laugh (but not at their own expense)
- a change of scenery
- going on a voyage
- meeting new people
- any conversation, chat or gossip
- to feel like a pioneer
- to discuss his or her emotions
- to eat at expensive restaurants

Dislikes

- silence
- schedules and timetables
- disapproval
- bureaucrats
- unenthusiastic or disinterested people
- uncommunicative people
- being told what to do
- having too many material possessions
- listening to others
- criticism or complaint
- solitude

GOOD FRIENDS FOR HORSES

The diagram below shows the compatibility of horse with other animals. There is no fixed ruling, however, because there are other influences on both the horse and any potential friend. These influences are:

- the companion in life (see pp. 23–25)
- the dominant element (from the year of birth)

Compatibility of horse		
▼ Rat	■ Dragon	▼ Monkey
○ Ox	○ Snake	● Rooster
▲ Tiger	■ Horse	▲ Dog
▼ Rabbit	▲ Goat	■ Pig

Key

▲ Highly compatible
● Amicable
■ No conflict but needs some effort
○ Lack of sympathy
▼ Antagonistic

Rat with horse This is a partnership definitely to be avoided. Horse and rat rub each other up the wrong way.

Ox with horse This will be an unhappy match for the pair. They will only annoy one another. Lively horse will not get any excitement from the ox; oxen cannot give the flattery that vain horses require. Also, horses are too free-thinking to accept the ox's authoritarian habits for long.

Tiger with horse There can be great attachment between a tiger and a horse. Patient horse will enjoy the company of energetic tiger and stick by him when he's down. Even so, they will probably argue and need to take time out from the relationship.

Rabbit with horse Moody horse makes a disruptive partner for rabbit, who may not tolerate this for long unless very much in love.

Dragon with horse Enthusiastic horse and energetic dragon can get on well together if they share a common purpose and the dragon does not invade the horse's privacy too much. Otherwise, daily life will split them up. Self-preoccupied horses are not able to give dragons the attention they need.

Snake with horse At first, there will be a mutual attraction of opposites between the out-going horse and the more reticent snake. The horse will soon tire of thoughtful snake who, in turn, will tire of horse's lack of mental concentration.

Horse with horse This is a potentially enjoyable combination but is likely to be unstable. Two restless horses may have a lot in common but they will find it doubly hard to settle down together.

Goat with horse Goats and horses complement each other. The goat will feel secure with horse but the relationship will still be exciting. Both are unstable and irresponsible people who dislike routine.

Monkey with horse A relationship between these two will be plagued by misunderstandings. Horse will find monkey's lively intelligence calculating; monkey will think the horse's enthusiasm is based on naivety or even stupidity.

Rooster with horse These two can get on quite well together. The horse will initiate things and the rooster can complete them. They are, however, both sensitive to the opinions of others while being tactless themselves. This could create problems and bruised egos

Dog with horse This is a case of opposites that attract. The horse appreciates the dog's loyal and generous nature and their ability to see things as they really are. In turn, dogs take great pleasure in the company of lively horses and will ignore their waywardness.

Pig with horse At first, these two can get along. The pig will find the horse exciting and the horse will enjoy pig's kind and loving nature. Eventually, however, selfish horse will test the pig's patience to the limit, or the horse will get bored with the pig.

HORSE IN LOVE

Horses love to be in love. In fact, they can be more in love with the idea of being in love than with the actual recipient of their affections. Horse people are the type to fall in love at first sight. Once smitten, they put all their energies into seducing that person. As partners, horses are exciting but difficult. They are moody and like their freedom while still demanding support. They are highly romantic and live at the mercy of their emotions. For love, a horse will change everything: move house, change job or emigrate, for example. They are flighty people, however, and will fall out of love as quickly as they fell in love. To keep horses interested, partners should try ignoring them. Any lasting relationship with a horse will be punctuated by major crises. Strangely enough, these actually help to prolong the relationship as they keep the horse interested – horse people thrive on dramatic scenes.

HORSE AND SEX

Horses are the epitome of sex appeal and are very sensual. A horse will be impatient to consummate a relationship and will employ whatever means are necessary to seduce the object of his or her passion. Horses are passionate and energetic lovers. They are sprinters, however, and not marathon runners, so don't expect all-night performances. Horses are enthusiastic about sex and expect their partners to share this. Their enthusiasm may quickly wane, however, as horses can run hot one minute and cold the next. Sadly, horses are likely to be unfaithful. They are generally weak people who cannot resist temptation. Unreasonably, perhaps, they will expect to be forgiven as easily as they forget. Usually, horse people's total immersion in love makes it easier for others to forgive their indiscretions and egocentric behaviour.

HEALTH

Horse's element, fire, is associated with the heart and small intestine, so horses should pay particular attention to keeping these organs in working order, in particular by watching their diets and establishing healthy eating patterns. Horses are highly strung and need to expend their energies in some kind of exertion. This nervous energy will otherwise affect the horse both physically and mentally, therefore making them prone to psychosomatic disorders – those brought about by mental stress – such as anxiety attacks, insomnia and eating disorders.

LEISURE INTERESTS

Horses enjoy all kinds of sport and especially competitive ones. Although they are not very good at cooperating, team sports such as football or hockey appeal to horses. This is because they allow the horse to shine while still providing the necessary support that the horse needs to succeed. Horses also love most outdoor pursuits – basically anything that gets them out of the house. On holiday, camping is enjoyed by horses as it allows them to feel independent and pioneering without actually being too daring. Hiking and canoeing appeal to their carefree natures.

THE HORSE YEARS AND THEIR ELEMENTS

The horse is a Yang fire animal. Each of the horse years, however, is associated with an element which is said to have its own influence. These elements are wood, fire, earth, metal and water. They influence horse in a regular sequence, which is repeated every 60 years. In the table below, for example, the horse year 1942 is a water year. The next horse water year is 60 years later in 2003, and the next will be 2063. Horse's natural element is fire; the influence of this combines with those of the element of the year of birth. The possible effects of the year elements are listed below.

Lunar years ruled by the horse and their elements		
1906	25 Jan 1906 – 12 Feb 1907	**fire**
1918	11 Feb 1918 – 31 Jan 1919	**earth**
1930	30 Jan 1930 – 16 Feb 1931	**metal**
1942	15 Feb 1942 – 4 Feb 1943	**water**
1954	3 Feb 1954 – 23 Jan 1955	**wood**
1966	21 Jan 1966 – 8 Feb 1967	**fire**
1978	7 Feb 1978 – 27 Jan 1979	**earth**
1990	27 Jan 1990 – 14 Feb 1991	**metal**
2002	12 Feb 2002 – 31 Jan 2003	**water**

Horse *Fire–Fire* (1906, 1966)

Fire horses are exceptional people. To be born during the year of the fire horse is considered either very advantageous or disastrous. In China, many people try to avoid giving birth during fire horse years as they do not want to risk bringing bad luck into the family. Fire multiplies both the good and bad attributes of the horse. These people are extreme and excessive. More adventurous, passionate, unruly and talented than other horses, they will lead thrilling lives. Fire horses are destined for great success or spectacular failure.

Horse *Fire–Earth* (1918, 1978)

Earth brings stability to the horse. The capability and resourcefulness of this element makes earth horses less flighty. They are more able to see a project through to the end. These horses are more responsible and cautious yet they are not as much fun as typical horses. Normally, earthy types are very conventional, but horse breathes fresh air into this element and prevents inflexibility. Earth horses will express their nervous energies by paying attention to details and by displaying minor eccentricities.

Horse *Fire–Metal* (1930, 1990)

Metal is quite a good element for horse. It compensates for some of the horse's failings. They can be more resolute and persevering than other horses – but only if they are motivated. Metal horses need a lot of stimulation to stop them getting bored. Metal horses are headstrong and irrepressible. Metal can also restrain horses, smothering their passionate natures. This is not necessarily a good thing as horses need to give vent to their emotions.

Horse *Fire–Water* (1942, 2002)

Water facilitates the horse's dormant creativity and brings these people success in the arts. Elusive water and easily distracted horse combine to produce people with very short attention spans. Water is a communicative element and enhances the horse's already verbose nature. It allows them to be humorous and witty in their conversation. Although inconsiderate and self-centred, water horses endear themselves to others by being charming. They cultivate daredevil personae that allow others to excuse their shortcomings. Water exploits the horse's nervous energy and these horses keep active and like to live by their wits.

Horse *Fire–Wood* (1954, 2014)

Wood has a calming influence on the horse. Wood horses are more cooperative and helpful than other horses. They should watch out for others trying to take advantage of them though, as wood diminishes the horse's perceptive abilities, making them too gullible at times. Wood helps to settle the horse's nervous energies. Emotionally, therefore, this horse is not so prone to depression and bad moods and will be mostly happy and good-tempered.

HORSE AND THE ZODIAC OF WESTERN ASTROLOGY

To work out your zodiac sign see p. 26–27. General character traits of horses of the 12 zodiac signs are given overleaf. Bear in mind that the Western zodiac sign modifies the basic horse nature – especially in the area of personal relationships.

Aries horse Aries exacerbates the horse's wild side. These horses are aggressively competitive and very enterprising. Aries horses are more capable of devotion than other horses and are good company.

Taurus horse Pragmatic Taurus allows the horse to plan ahead. These horses are less temperamental and more stable but they can be too rigid. Taurean horses are not averse to taking advice from others.

Gemini horse These two signs share many similar traits which are therefore multiplied under this sign. Gemini horses are even more enthusiastic, curious, rebellious and sociable than usual.

Cancer horse Cancer makes this horse able to appreciate the needs and wishes of others. Being more sensitive, these horses are very dependent on the love and support of close family and friends.

Leo horse To these horses, the world is their playground. The Leo horse loves adventure, craves admiration and is not beset by the self-doubts that normally plague the horse.

Virgo horse Virgoan horses are well-balanced people. Virgo cures some of the horse's shortcomings, such as lack of precision, lack of self-discipline, irresponsibility and unruliness.

Libra horse Libran horses are level-headed and realistic yet surprisingly indecisive. Not as independent as other horses, they are honest about how important their loved ones are to them.

Scorpio horse Headstrong, stubborn and wild, these horses never compromise. They direct their considerable energies into fulfilling their desires – which govern the lives of Scorpio horses.

Sagittarius horse The symbol of Sagittarius is itself a horse. In many ways, these people are almost stereotypical horses. Easy-going and carefree, they are fun people but typically unpredictable.

Capricorn horse Capricorn makes these horses relatively materialistic. A Capricorn horse is not afraid of working hard to achieve financial security. They are more serious in their demeanour than one would expect from a horse.

Aquarius horse Two unpredictable signs combine to produce an eccentric but talented horse. More than any other horses, Aquarian horses love the company of new friends.

Pisces horse Self-conscious Pisces heightens the horse's basic insecurities. When they are not being anxious, Piscean horses are loving, eager to please and warm-hearted.

Some famous people born in the years of the horse and their zodiac signs

- **Rembrandt**
  Painter
  15 Jul 1606 Cancer

- **Isaac Newton**
  Scientist
  25 Dec 1642 Capricorn

- **Antonio Vivaldi**
  Composer
  4 Mar 1678 Pisces

- **Davy Crockett**
  Frontiersman
  17 Aug 1786 Leo

- **Frédéric Chopin**
  Composer
  22 Feb 1810 Pisces

- **Edgar Dégas**
  Artist
  19 Jul 1834 Cancer

- **Giacomo Puccini**
  Composer
  22 Dec 1858 Capricorn

- **Vladimir Lenin**
  Political leader
  4 Mar 1870 Pisces

- **Igor Stravinsky**
  Composer
  17 Jun 1882 Gemini

- **Otto Preminger**
  Film director
  5 Dec 1906 Sagittarius

- **Ella Fitzgerald**
  Singer
  25 Apr 1918 Taurus

- **Rita Hayworth**
  Actress
  17 Oct 1918 Libra

- **Alexander Solzhenitsyn**
  Novelist
  11 Dec 1918 Sagittarius

- **Clint Eastwood**
  Actor
  31 May 1930 Gemini

- **Ted Hughes**
  Poet
  16 Aug 1930 Leo

- **Sean Connery**
  Actor
  25 Aug 1930 Virgo

- **Ray Charles**
  Singer
  23 Sep 1930 Libra

- **Barbra Streisand**
  Actress/Singer
  24 Apr 1942 Taurus

- **Paul McCartney**
  Musician/Songwriter
  18 Jun 1942 Gemini

- **Jimi Hendrix**
  Rock singer
  27 Nov 1942 Sagittarius

8. The Goat
The Yin fire animal

Lunar years ruled by the goat			
1907	13 Feb 1907	–	1 Feb 1908
1919	1 Feb 1919	–	19 Feb 1920
1931	17 Feb 1931	–	5 Feb 1932
1943	5 Feb 1943	–	24 Jan 1944
1955	24 Jan 1955	–	11 Feb 1956
1967	9 Feb 1967	–	29 Jan 1968
1979	28 Jan 1979	–	15 Feb 1980
1991	15 Feb 1991	–	3 Feb 1992
2003	1 Feb 2003	–	21 Jan 2004

The goat is associated with harmony, creativity, peace and pleasure. In China, the goat is seen as a harbinger of peace.

THE GOAT PERSONALITY

Charming, amiable and sympathetic, goats are genuinely nice people. They hate to criticize and always look for the best in people – including themselves. A goat will prefer to forget grievances rather than brood over them and will bottle up resentments to keep the peace. Goat people live in the present, which they enjoy to the best of their abilities. Thanks to their sensitive natures, goats are one of the most artistic and creative of all the Chinese horoscope signs.

CHARACTERISTICS

These are the general personality traits of those people who are typical goats, both at their best and at their worst.

Positive	Negative
● creative	● eccentric
● imaginative	● illogical
● ingenious	● vulnerable
● honest	● irresponsible
● capricious	● irrational
● sensitive	● naive
● faithful	● unsatisfied
● sincere	● disorganized
● peaceful	● impulsive
● adaptable	● lazy
● independent	● gullible
● ardent	● indulgent
● elegant	● careless
● gentle	● anxious
● easy-going	● impractical

SECRET GOAT

From their description, people may think that goats are weak creatures who are easy to take advantage of. In reality, however, they will fight violently if something important to them is threatened. Fortunately, as goats apportion value according to very personal criteria, what they would defend to the last is not often something that others covet.

ELEMENT

Goat is linked to the ancient Chinese element of fire. Fire is a dynamic, exciting and energetic sign. In the case of goats, fire expresses itself in their imaginative and creative abilities. Normally, fire people are as fiery as the sign suggests. The easy-going and carefree nature of the goat, however, dampens their fiery sides, which are kept well hidden until times of crisis.

BALANCE

Normally, people are advised to look to themselves to balance the strengths and weaknesses of their characters. For example, the goat would be advised to try and take more care of the practical side of life – such as paying the bills – and not rely on others to support them as they pursue their own interests. Chinese tradition, however, holds that goats are mostly unable to change this aspect of their natures. Therefore, they will need to find a patron to take care of the 'administration' of their life and allow them the freedom to make the most of their creative talents. This role could be filled by, for example, a devoted husband or wife, a manager or even a loyal accountant!

Traditionally, the following are said to be associated with goats:

Taste	bitter
Season	summer
Birth	rainy day
Colours	sky-blue
Plant	wormwood, anise
Flower	honeysuckle
Food	rice, lamb
Climate	hot

THE MALE GOAT

If a man has a typical goat personality, he will generally display the behaviour listed below.

- is dependent on his family
- will be a fun but irresponsible parent
- is fretful and indecisive
- has a highly developed aesthetic sense
- is unusually sensitive for a man
- has a natural flair for hospitality
- is reflective and gentle
- will remember birthdays and anniversaries
- is easily put off by obstacles

THE FEMALE GOAT

If a woman has a typical goat personality, she will generally display the behaviour listed below.

- is indifferent to conventions
- is angered by injustice
- is talented
- leads a carefree existence
- is never hostile
- is impressionable and easily led
- likes to be the centre of attention
- fears rejection and criticism
- needs security to blossom
- likes to be noticed

THE GOAT CHILD

If a child has a typical goat personality, he or she will generally display the behaviour listed below.

- is delicate and sickly
- needs to be indulged
- is inconstant and unstable
- is timid and uncertain at times
- blossoms with a supportive family
- must be allowed to find their own way
- enjoys creating things
- makes up fantasies and fairy tales
- will give away their toys to friends

GOAT AT HOME

Goats love the creature comforts of life but are not practical enough to go out and get them. It is usually left to their partner or family to decorate and furnish the home. Nonetheless, goats are very acquisitive – they are attracted to beautiful or novel things. A goat house will be full of knick-knacks, souvenirs and odd bits of furniture that have caught the goat's fancy. They love junk shops, charity shops and markets where they can find new and interesting goods at low prices. If they have enough money, they will indulge themselves by rummaging round the better department stores as if they were jumble sales. At heart though, goats are indifferent to material possessions and will be as happy in another's home that is full of beautiful objects as their own. A goat may have one beautiful item, perhaps made by themselves, installed in their home that negates the drab surroundings.

GOAT AT WORK

Goats would never work if they had the choice, if only money was not a necessity. They are not especially active or hard-working and will be lazy and erratic at work. Despite this, if goats do undertake a job then they will carry it out properly or not at all. Goats can be both scrupulous and perfectionists. They have a profiteering side and hate to support themselves – they will try to profit from the hard work of others. This does not mean that they are ambitious, as they will not better themselves at the expense of others. If they do have some money, goats will be better off seeking advice on how to invest it wisely rather than using it to start their own business. Goats are inspired by the arts and love anything concerned with harmony and beauty. They come into their own in art if they have a mentor or patron who can recognize and encourage their talents.

Some typical goat occupations

- actor/actress
- story writer
- painter
- musician
- landscape gardener
- weaver
- potter
- courtesan

- television presenter
- gigolo
- dancer
- tramp!
- fortune teller
- escort
- investor
- shareholder

GOAT PREFERENCES

Likes

- to please others
- beauty
- to make people curious
- tranquillity
- to forgive and forget
- parks with fountains
- marble statues
- costume dramas
- to be taken care of
- beautiful people

Dislikes

- to be made to choose
- unwanted responsibility
- routines
- to be involved in others' problems
- obligations
- hostile atmospheres
- to offend others
- emotional scenes
- doing the accounts
- taking the initiative

GOOD FRIENDS FOR GOATS

The diagram below shows the compatibility of goat with other animals. There is no fixed ruling, however, because there are other influences on both the goat and any potential friend. These influences are:

- the companion in life (see pp. 23–25)
- the dominant element (from the year of birth)

Compatibility of goat with other animals		
○ Rat	○ Dragon	● Monkey
○ Ox	● Snake	○ Rooster
■ Tiger	▲ Horse	■ Dog
▲ Rabbit	● Goat	▲ Pig

Key

▲ Highly compatible
● Amicable
■ No conflict but needs some effort
○ Lack of sympathy
▼ Antagonistic

Rat with goat There is not much mutual understanding between these two but they are fine together for short periods for specific interests. In general, carefree goat will be good for rat, and enjoy rat's charm.

Ox with goat Goats and oxen have discordant personalities. Goat's habit of acting without thinking will only annoy careful ox. They also have different priorities in life: goat is too capricious and ox demands fidelity as the basis for a relationship.

Tiger with goat Difficult, but potentially mutually rewarding. Goat will admire tiger's nerve and loyalty while tiger will appreciate goat's fun-loving nature. To be more than fair-weather friends, however, a little effort will be needed.

Rabbit with goat This may be the best match as both have good taste and a love of luxuries in common. Goat's imaginative nature appeals to rabbit's romantic side. In difficult times, however, neither will be able to look to the other for courage and support as both are anxious creatures.

Dragon with goat A lack of understanding can blight any relationship between these two, unless they both learn to accept and appreciate their differences. Business alliances will be more successful than personal ones as dragons can help quiet goats realize their creativity.

Snake with goat Both goat and snake love art, beauty and harmony. As long as life is good, these two will rarely argue as it is too much trouble. Otherwise, goat may find snake too serious and snake will think goat weak.

Horse with goat Goats and horses complement each other. The goat will feel secure with horse but the relationship will still be exciting, as both are unstable and irresponsible people who dislike routine.

Goat with goat Two goats can have an idyllic relationship if they have enough money to not worry about paying the bills. Otherwise, neither can rely on the other for moral support. They can be friends only if they apply their tolerant natures to ignoring the other's faults.

Monkey with goat Goat and monkey will never be bored together. With monkey's quick wits and goat's imagination there will always be plenty to do and they can be great friends. As lovers, monkeys may not be able to provide the constant reassurances that goats need.

Rooster with goat These two have very little in common and do not understand each other. Although rooster will be able to support goat financially, goat will not give rooster moral support in return.

Dog with goat Goat and dog can be friends if they apply their tolerant natures to ignoring the other's differences. Normally, however, whimsical goat and realistic dog just irritate each other.

Pig with goat This is a good alliance for both signs. Both value tranquillity and harmony, and are able to make the concessions necessary to achieve them. Goat should take care not to stretch the pig's tolerance too far, however, by acting too irresponsibly.

GOAT IN LOVE

Goats cannot be objective and they think that the world revolves around them and their loved ones. Effectively it does, as they will simply blinker themselves to matters not concerning them. Emotional and sensitive, goats have great expectations of romance but they will also give a lot in return. A goat will adapt to please a loved one and does not mind making concessions to keep the peace. They are polite and affectionate partners. Although goats are sympathetic, they are not particularly compassionate, so partners should not expect to burden the goat with their problems. Goats do not like to be depended on. Conversely, the goat will expect their partner to be always there for them and to be never even tempted by another. Above all else, partners must accept goats as they are and not try to change them.

GOAT AND SEX

Goats are curious rather than passionate people. They cannot be logical or objective about their emotions. To a goat, feelings and emotions are as important as the sexual act itself. They are not capable of one-night stands and will be hurt and confused if they embark on a physical relationship only to find the other person does not feel anything for them. Goats begin sexual relationships with delicacy and elegance. They love long drawn-out seductions with all the trimmings of romance. The subtleties and game-play of courtships intrigue them. Initially, though, they may be timid and uncertain with new lovers. Goats are not demanding lovers provided they think they are the only one for their mate.

HEALTH

Goat's element, fire, is associated with the heart and small intestine, so goats should pay particular attention to keeping these organs in working order. Being of the Yin tendency, goats are advised to try and prevent, rather than cure, illnesses. It is probably the case that most goats, being nervous of their health, are already practising this by having regular check-ups with the doctor. Yin people tend to have delicate constitutions. Goats should make sure they keep warm during the winter months and remember to relax occasionally. Meditation would probably be beneficial for goats as it would help them focus their energies and develop an inner sense of wellbeing.

LEISURE INTERESTS

Goats are not particularly energetic people. They would rather visit an art gallery than go swimming. Parks, botanical gardens, historic houses and flower gardens will all have many goat visitors. Goats love anything in which they can find beauty and harmony. Alternatively, goats spend a lot of their time visiting friends. They are never short of invitations as goat people bring a pleasant ambience to any gathering. On the whole, goats are better as guests than hosts. As guests they only have to be their agreeable selves, but as hosts they would have to organize and plan the event – not goat strong points.

THE GOAT YEARS AND THEIR ELEMENTS

The goat is a Yin fire animal. Each of the goat years, however, is associated with an element which is said to have its own influence. These elements are wood, fire, earth, metal and water. They influence goat in a regular sequence, which is repeated every 60 years. In the table below, for example, the goat year 1907 is a fire year. The next goat fire year is 60 years later in 1967, and the next will be 2027. Goat's natural element is fire; the influence of this combines with those of the element of the year of birth. The possible effects of the year elements are listed below.

Lunar years ruled by the goat and their elements		
1901 19 Feb 1901	–	7 Feb 1902 **metal**
1913 6 Feb 1913	–	25 Jan 1914 **water**
1925 25 Jan 1925	–	12 Feb 1926 **wood**
1937 11 Feb 1937	–	30 Jan 1938 **fire**
1949 29 Jan 1949	–	16 Feb 1950 **earth**
1961 15 Feb 1961	–	4 Feb 1962 **metal**
1973 3 Feb 1973	–	22 Jan 1974 **water**
1985 20 Feb 1985	–	8 Feb 1986 **wood**
1997 8 Feb 1997	–	27 Jan 1998 **fire**

Goat *Fire–Fire* (1907, 1967)

Fire is the goat's natural element. Double fire goats are blessed with courage and intuition. These goats are dramatic and innovative, yet they have a knack of making their wild ideas seem safe and logical. They do, however, have a tendency to be reckless and of not looking before they leap. Goats are never very good at managing their money, and double fire goats are even worse. Money almost burns holes in their pockets. As with all fire types, these goats are attractive and appealing people. They are gentle and sympathetic but intolerant of those they consider fools.

Goat *Fire–Wood* (1955, 2015)

Wood is a creative element associated with growth, renewal and innovation. Combined with the goat's imagination, this makes wood goats highly artistic. It also heightens the goat's sensitive nature. Unlike water goats, however, wood makes goats very compassionate people and not worriers. These people are generous with their time and money for good causes that they believe in; but they are more likely to be working in the local charity shop than far away in a refugee camp.

Goat *Fire–Earth* (1919, 1979)

Earth grounds the goat. It brings them down to earth and keeps their heads out of the clouds for too long. Earth bestows steadfastness and the ability to work hard on the goat. These goats are more materialistic than the rest of the breed. Atypically, earth goats are capable of fulfilling their own material needs and are not so dependent on others to organize them. Earth goats are basically cheerful and optimistic people but when wronged they can complain too much. Earth signs can, at times, be so cautious and practical that they stagnate.

Goat *Fire–Metal* (1931, 1991)

Metal strengthens the goat. It brings determination and perseverance to an otherwise work-shy type of person. Fire combines with metal to give these people more presence than typical goats. Metal goats are still sensitive but not as vulnerable as usual. In fact, other people do not realize how sensitive and affectionate these goats really are underneath their harsh exteriors. As with all metal types, these are very ambitious people; but their ambitions will be directed towards typically goat-like goals – achieving in the arts, for example.

Goat *Fire–Water* (1943, 2003)

Fluid water makes the goat even more capricious than usual. Water goats are incredibly sensitive people and very perceptive emotionally. This can hamper them as they will internalize other people's problems and may become worriers. Fire aligned with water makes these people able to get their own way – but very subtly. Surprisingly, water goats are conservative people; they are fearful of change and do not like to take risks.

GOAT AND THE ZODIAC OF WESTERN ASTROLOGY

To work out your zodiac sign see p. 27. General character traits of goats of the 12 zodiac signs are given below. Bear in mind that the Western zodiac sign modifies the basic goat nature – especially in the area of personal relationships.

Aries goat The goat and the ram share many traits. So those born under both these signs are almost stereotypical goats. Yet they are more independent and are even headstrong. Aries makes the goat stubborn and, unlike other goats, these people hold grudges and will exact revenge on their enemies.

Taurus goat Taurean goats crave domestic and financial security. They are cautious and never take risks. Although still easy-going, if pushed to the limit a Taurus goat will soon break into a fury.

Gemini goat Mercurial Gemini and capricious goat combine to make easily-distracted people. They are intelligent and curious and always have something on their minds.

Cancer goat Moody Cancer serves to make the goat temperamental as well as inconstant. These goats are very concerned about what others think of them. If they feel secure, then Cancerian goats will be kind and gentle; if they feel neglected, they can be vindictive and stubborn.

Leo goat Leo brings a much-needed measure of common sense to the goat. Leo goats are both sensitive and resolute. They are the most charismatic of all the goats and it is easy for them to find willing supporters of their latest idea or scheme.

Virgo goat Virgo goats are perfectionists and apply this in their drive to help others. Although they can be too critical, Virgoan goats are basically well-meaning. They are more intellectual than other goats and need a job that exploits this to prevent boredom.

Libra goat Libra goats are intelligent and refined. They like to make a good impression and will take care of their appearance. Capable of making great compromises to keep people's affection, these goats need constant companionship.

Scorpio goat Scorpio endows the goat with huge reserves of willpower. Their sensitive natures take second place to their ambitions. Yet these goats are not practical. They are erratic and eccentric but have bursts of wisdom and are very gifted artistically.

Sagittarius goat Sagittarian goats have enough self-confidence to support themselves and do not need to look for others to care for them. They are more adventurous yet less sensitive than other goats.

Capricorn goat Capricorn goats are practical and opportunistic. Financial wealth and status are important to them and they are usually successful in their chosen careers. These goats do find it difficult to be open emotionally with others though.

Aquarius goat Visionary Aquarius and imaginative goat combine to give great potential. These people are gifted planners, oblivious to criticism and often idiosyncratic. Aquarian goats are innovative but need to learn to evaluate risks.

Pisces goat Born under two sensitive signs, Pisces goats are almost too sensitive for their own good. Their emotions will reflect the atmosphere of their surroundings. These goats are inspired people but need a stable home base before they can express their creativity.

Some famous people born in the years of the goat and their zodiac signs

- **Michelangelo**
  Artist
  6 Mar 1475 Pisces

- **Jane Austen**
  Novelist
  16 Dec 1775 Sagittarius

- **Alexander Pushkin**
  Writer
  6 Jun 1799 Gemini

- **Mark Twain**
  Writer
  30 Nov 1835 Sagittarius

- **Arthur Conan Doyle**
  Novelist
  22 May 1859 Gemini

- **Marcel Proust**
  Novelist
  10 Jul 1871 Cancer

- **Benito Mussolini**
  Dictator
  29 Jul 1883 Leo

- **Coco Chanel**
  Fashion designer
  19 Aug 1883 Leo

- **Rudolph Valentino**
  Actor
  6 May 1895 Taurus

- **Laurence Olivier**
  Actor
  22 May 1907 Gemini

- **Simone de Beauvoir**
  Novelist
  9 Jan 1908 Capricorn

- **Margot Fonteyn**
  Ballerina
  18 May 1919 Taurus

- **Doris Lessing**
  Novelist
  22 Oct 1919 Libra

- **Anne Bancroft**
  Actress
  17 Sep 1931 Virgo

- **John Le Carré**
  Novelist
  19 Oct 1931 Libra

- **Mick Jagger**
  Rock singer
  26 Jul 1943 Leo

- **Robert de Niro**
  Actor
  17 Aug 1943 Leo

- **Chevy Chase**
  Actor
  8 Oct 1943 Libra

- **Catherine Deneuve**
  Actress
  22 Oct 1943 Libra

- **John Denver**
  Singer
  31 Dec 1943 Capricorn

9. The Monkey
The Yang metal animal

Lunar years ruled by the monkey			
1908	2 Feb 1908	–	21 Jan 1909
1920	20 Feb 1920	–	7 Feb 1921
1932	6 Feb 1932	–	25 Jan 1933
1944	25 Jan 1944	–	12 Feb 1945
1956	12 Feb 1956	–	30 Jan 1957
1968	30 Jan 1968	–	16 Feb 1969
1980	16 Feb 1980	–	4 Feb 1981
1992	4 Feb 1992	–	22 Jan 1993
2004	22 Jan 2004	–	8 Feb 2005

In some parts of China, the monkey is worshipped as the 'Great Sage Equal to Heaven'. Monkeys are also associated with adultery, justice and, emotionally, with sorrow.

THE MONKEY PERSONALITY

Highly competitive and insatiably curious, monkeys are very shrewd. They are intelligent and ingenious and try to make the best of any situation. Monkeys are quick-witted and never at a loss for words. They have a reputation for trickery. Although monkeys can be scheming and are good at manipulating people, they use these skills wisely. Despite this, monkeys are quick to stop others manipulating them. Monkeys try to be honest but will tell a lie if it is convenient.

CHARACTERISTICS

These are the general personality traits of those people who are typical monkeys, both at their best and worst.

Positive	Negative
● independent	● opportunistic
● astute	● restless
● sociable	● manipulative
● vivacious	● scheming
● enthusiastic	● unpredictable
● tolerant	● secretive
● lively	● deceitful
● quick-witted	● mischievous
● sensitive	● vain
● generous	● fickle
● optimistic	● dishonest
● entertaining	● selfish
● audacious	● cunning
● gregarious	● opinionated
● inventive	● devious

SECRET MONKEY

In public, monkeys always appear light-hearted and carefree. In private, however, they may be nursing deep feelings of insecurity. Monkeys get very hurt if they feel rejected or shut out – but they will make light of the situation and cover their true feelings.

ELEMENT

Monkey is linked to the ancient Chinese element of metal. This is a very strong element. It can be seen positively as a valuable resource, such as gold; or negatively as a weapon, such as a sword. In monkeys, the energy of metal expresses itself as their imaginative, ambitious and independent streaks.

BALANCE

Monkeys are curious people, who find something of interest anywhere. They are attracted to the new and unknown. This can make them broad-minded and knowledgeable people, but their energies can be dissipated by these many interests. Monkeys need to learn how to channel their energies into one particular goal at a time. If they can balance their need to search for fresh pastures by bringing some routine or stability into their life, they will find that they can achieve considerable success.

BEST ASSOCIATIONS

Traditionally, the following are said to be associated with monkeys:

Taste	pungent
Season	autumn
Birth	summer
Colours	white
Plants	Chinese wolfberry
Flowers	bird of paradise
Food	cloves
Climate	dry

THE MALE MONKEY

If a man has a typical monkey personality, he will generally display the behaviour listed below.

- breaks the rules
- lacks self-discipline
- likes to gamble
- is accommodating
- appears to be shallow
- is very good with children
- gets on well with women
- likes to tease his friends
- can lie cheerfully
- is warm-hearted and generous
- has a sharp sense of humour

THE FEMALE MONKEY

If a woman has a typical monkey personality, she will generally display the behaviour listed below.

- provokes jealousy
- is flirtatious
- needs to be independent
- is witty
- likes to have her own space
- prefers not to marry
- is very good with children
- does not have conventional morals
- is more honest than the male
- is very practical
- is good at fixing things

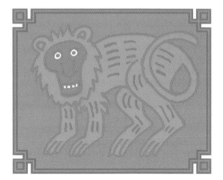

THE MONKEY CHILD

If a child has a typical monkey personality, he or she will generally display the behaviour listed below.

- has a tendency to become overexcited
- needs to be encouraged to calm down
- is impatient and hot-tempered
- has a lively imagination
- adapts easily to new environments
- is very critical of peers
- will not suffer bullying for long
- has a short attention span
- can stand up for himself or herself

MONKEY AT HOME

Monkeys are not stay-at-home types. Nevertheless, a stable home environment is important. It gives them a sound base from which to venture forth on their latest adventure. Monkeys hate the status quo. They will always be planning to move to a better house or, if this is not possible, then they will be organizing a major redecoration of their home. Monkeys are real DIY enthusiasts; they are practical people and enjoy making, repairing and decorating. Even when restricted by funds, a monkey will find ingenious ways to furnish and decorate a house. For example, tables and chairs will be made from odds and ends and lots of brightly coloured objects of interest displayed as ornaments.

MONKEY AT WORK

Monkeys can always find work as they are versatile and quick-thinking. They are highly flexible people who can turn their hand to virtually anything. Monkeys hate routine. For monkeys to stay in a job, it must provide them with plenty of variety as well as challenge. If they are overstimulated, however, their minds will wander. When this happens, or alternatively, if they are bored, the monkey's notoriously short attention span will cause them to change career. Also, a monkey will feel trapped in a predictable career. So, one year a monkey may be teaching English and the next driving a bus. Whatever their job though, monkeys are at their best when they are breaking or stretching the rules. To be happy at work, monkeys need a position where they are allowed to use their discretion and need to use their wits.

Some typical monkey occupations

- counsellor
- therapist
- installation artist
- bus driver
- occupational therapist
- nurse
- judo instructor
- English teacher
- art critic
- stockbroker
- theologian
- foreign correspondent
- town planner
- writer
- journalist

MONKEY PREFERENCES

Likes

- a challenge
- to listen to other's problems and worries
- to care for people
- casting horoscopes
- alternative belief systems
- to travel
- practical jokes
- decorating their house
- reading tarot cards
- visiting friends
- ethnic art
- games of chance
- nightclubs

Dislikes

- routine
- pubs and alcohol
- established religions
- being manipulated
- depending on others
- doing without money
- purely physical work
- the achievements of others
- conventional people
- compromising their independence

GOOD FRIENDS FOR MONKEYS

The diagram below shows the compatibility of monkey with other animals. There is no fixed ruling, however, because there are other influences on both the monkey and any potential friend. These influences are:

- the companion in life (see pp. 23–25)
- the dominant element (from the year of birth)

Compatibility of monkey with other animals

▲ Rat	▲ Dragon	○ Monkey
■ Ox	▼ Snake	■ Rooster
▼ Tigor	◡ Horse	● Dog
○ Rabbit	● Goat	● Pig

Key

▲ Highly compatible

● Amicable

■ No conflict but needs some effort

○ Lack of sympathy

▼ Antagonistic

Rat with monkey An entertaining but cunning pair. On the whole, this combination will last because they have much in common. Rat may have to accept monkey's dominance.

Ox with monkey Mischievous monkey will tease the serious ox, but gently and with love. Oxen are fascinated by the monkey's sparkling personality but these two are unlikely to settle down together. They may misunderstand each other and monkey will not hang around long enough to sort out any differences.

Tiger with monkey Tiger and monkey are both competitive and neither knows how to compromise. Secretly, monkeys may admire tigers, but cannot resist mocking them; tigers cannot help retaliating, and the relationship could quickly become destructive. Unless there is great love on monkey's part and moderation on tiger's part, no relationship will work.

Rabbit with monkey Devious monkey can bring out the worst, cunning side of rabbit. But as lively monkey finds stable rabbit dull, they are not often together long enough for this to happen.

Dragon with monkey Dragon is attracted by monkey's charm and intelligence. The two inspire and complement each other without becoming rivals – they will have many friends and a busy social life. Others may find them superficial, but they will be immune to criticism.

Snake with monkey Monkey is intelligent in a quick-witted sort of way, snake in a more profound fashion. This can lead to competition or a perfect business relationship. In love, however, monkey finds snake boring and will not settle down.

Horse with monkey A relationship between these two will be plagued by misunderstandings. Horse will find monkey's lively intelligence calculating; monkey will think horse's enthusiasm is based on naivety or even stupidity.

Goat with monkey A goat and a monkey will never be bored together. With monkey's quick wits and goat's imagination there will always be plenty to do and they can be great friends. As lovers, monkeys may not be able to provide the constant reassurances that goats need.

Monkey with monkey Monkey relishes the company of another monkey. They can appreciate the other's intelligence and audacity. The two could quickly become rivals though, as they are both competitive types. Unless they can communicate calmly, they will taunt each other with constant cynicism.

Rooster with monkey Clever monkey and frank rooster can work well together. Yet they will judge each other on appearance alone and both will find the other superficial. If they can learn not to criticize, these two can make a handsome and sociable couple.

Dog with monkey These two can be great friends. Dog is attracted by monkey's liveliness and the monkey appreciates dog's stability and broad-mindedness. Although there will be a good mutual understanding, both are cynical and the idealistic dog will be suspicious of realistic monkey's motives.

Pig with monkey As both are outgoing and friendly, this can be a well-balanced relationship. Monkey can help curb generous pig's excessive spending. Honest pig can appreciate monkey's plans and schemes.

MONKEY IN LOVE

Monkeys approach love in their typically vivacious and enthusiastic way. In the beginning, they are heady with passion and will be infatuated with their new-found love. As the novelty wears off, however, their excitement fades and monkeys may instead start to criticize their partner. The relationship has to be lively to keep a monkey interested. If happy and stimulated, a monkey can be a tolerant and understanding partner, although tears are just as likely as laughter in a relationship with a monkey – they are excitable and unpredictable people. Monkeys are usually charming and love to please. In return, they expect their partner to be alert and attentive to their needs.

MONKEY AND SEX

Not at all prudish, monkeys have healthy appetites for sex. They are inventive and imaginative lovers. Even so, it is important that a monkey's lover is entertaining company as well as passionate in bed. Monkeys soon tire of purely physical relationships. Unless they are well balanced, monkeys have a problem with fidelity. Always believing that the grass is greener on the other side of the fence, they have trouble appreciating what they already have. At the first sign of trouble, the instinct of a monkey is to run rather than to stay and sort it out.

HEALTH

Monkey's element, metal, is associated with the lungs and large intestine, so monkeys should pay particular attention to keeping these organs in working order. Also, monkeys should take care of their kidneys by not consuming too much coffee and salt. Despite the fact that they are not great athletes or keep-fit fans, monkeys are usually surprisingly fit and healthy people well into their old age. They tend to be naturally slight people. Monkeys should not neglect their diets – either through distraction or illness – as they may become too thin.

LEISURE INTERESTS

The leisure interests of monkeys are typically varied. Friendly and gregarious, monkeys inevitably spend a lot of time socializing. Either visiting or entertaining at home, a monkey can always be found at the hub of any social activity. For entertainment, they like to see the latest film or play the latest game. Monkeys like games of chance but will probably cheat! For exercise, they are attracted to all sports that involve speed, and especially water sports. Monkeys indulge their taste for the unusual and the exotic by visiting exhibitions of art from different cultures. Many monkeys are keen amateur photographers. This gives them an excuse to explore new places and acts as a cover for their curious natures.

THE MONKEY YEARS AND THEIR ELEMENTS

The monkey is a Yang metal animal. Each of the monkey years, however, is associated with an element which is said to have its own influence. These elements are wood, fire, earth, metal and water. They influence monkey in a regular sequence, which is repeated every 60 years. In the table below, for example, the monkey year 1908 is an earth year. The next monkey earth year is 60 years later in 1968, and the next will be 2028. Monkey's natural element is metal; the influence of this combines with those of the element of the year of birth. The possible effects of the year elements are listed below.

Lunar years ruled by the monkey and their elements

1908	2 Feb 1908	– 21 Jan 1909	**earth**
1920	20 Feb 1920	– 7 Feb 1921	**metal**
1932	6 Feb 1932	– 25 Jan 1933	**water**
1944	25 Jan 1944	– 12 Feb 1945	**wood**
1956	12 Feb 1956	– 30 Jan 1957	**fire**
1968	30 Jan 1968	– 16 Feb 1969	**earth**
1980	16 Feb 1980	– 4 Feb 1981	**metal**
1992	4 Feb 1992	– 22 Jan 1993	**water**
2004	22 Jan 2004	– 8 Feb 2005	**wood**

Monkey *Metal–Earth* (1908, 1968)

Earth is a sympathetic and balancing element for the metal-dominated monkey. It grounds these otherwise flighty people. Atypically, earth monkeys are studious, dutiful, hard-working and thorough. They are patient and scientific in their approach to solving problems. Earth enhances the monkey's natural intelligence, making them more intellectual. Earth monkeys have cutting tongues. They can be harsh in their criticisms of others. For this reason, these monkeys may have difficulties in their personal relationships.

Monkey *Metal–Metal* (1920, 1980)

Metal is the monkey's natural element. Double metal multiplies the monkey's intelligence but also increases aggressiveness. Metal monkeys are extremely independent people, simply because they feel superior to their peers. Metal monkeys are materialistic and, fortunately, have a knack for making money. With their nerves of steel, metal monkeys like to take risks and can be successful gamblers as they are fortunate people.

Monkey *Metal–Water* (1932, 1992)

Water and metal is a harmonious combination. Water monkeys are cooperative and understanding people. They are almost too sensitive and will see implied criticism where none is meant. Water enhances the monkey's already gregarious nature. Yet water monkeys are complex characters. Enigmatic and secretive, they keep their true feelings well hidden. These monkeys are prone to mood swings and are notoriously fickle.

Monkey *Metal–Wood* (1944, 2004)
Wood is a fortunate element for monkeys. It helps to
focus and stabilize them. Wood monkeys are friendly
and approachable people. Coupled with metal, wood
makes the monkey very resourceful and a great
problem-solver. In fact, wood monkeys are remarkable
people. Wood is a creative element, so monkeys born
in these years are likely to be artistic. They are also
gifted communicators who have a strong sense of
ethics.

Monkey *Metal–Fire* (1956, 2016)
Strong metal combined with passionate fire creates
powerful and dominant but aggressive people. Fire
also makes this monkey the most competitive of all
monkeys. They are driven to succeed. Yet fire and
metal brings conflict to the monkey. Fire monkeys
have great potential but they tend to overstretch
themselves. They do not always respond to challenges
in the best way. These monkeys need to accept their
own limitations and act accordingly.

MONKEY AND THE ZODIAC OF WESTERN ASTROLOGY

To work out your zodiac sign see p. 26–27.
General character traits of monkeys of the 12 zodiac
signs are given below. Bear in mind that the Western
zodiac sign modifies the basic monkey nature –
especially in the area of personal relationships.

Aries monkey Aries monkeys are some of the most talkative and forthright people around. They are uncannily perceptive and people can always recall the words of an Aries monkey. Both enterprising and opportunistic, they are also very successful.

Taurus monkey Determined Taurus facilitates the monkey's remarkable mental abilities. These people are capable and resourceful. Unusually persevering, they can apply themselves successfully to one task at a time.

Gemini monkey Mercurial Gemini and the trickster monkey have a lot in common. People born under both these signs are incredibly quick-witted but lack focus and direction. They are the mental gymnasts of the Chinese zodiac.

Cancer monkey Cancer brings extra sensitivity to the monkey. In fact, Cancer monkeys are moody as well as unpredictable. If they feel secure, then they can become more like the typical, happy-go-lucky monkey personality.

Leo monkey Leo monkeys are direct and candid people. They are very witty and are great raconteurs. Happy when they are the centre of attention, Leo monkeys get irritable when they are ignored.

Virgo monkey Analytical Virgo and clever monkey combine to make very profound people. Virgo monkeys can be too calculating and emotionally distant, however. Busy looking for hidden agendas, they can miss the more obvious facts.

Libra monkey Eloquent and sociable, these monkeys have the 'gift of the gab'. They pride themselves on their ability to get on with anyone. But Libran monkeys can be manipulative and tend to exploit weaker people.

Scorpio monkey Mystery-loving Scorpio and devious monkey are a dangerous combination. They are secretive people who are suspicious of everyone. Always planning and scheming, these monkeys assume that others are equally ambitious.

Sagittarius monkey Sagittarian monkeys are almost stereotypical monkeys. They are broad-minded and curious people. They love to travel and explore new horizons. If they are not stimulated, these monkeys will act mischievously.

Capricorn monkey This sign brings conflict to the monkey. Austere Capricorn and witty monkey combine to produce seemingly debonair people. In fact, Capricornean monkeys are often hiding great personal anguish beneath their smooth exteriors.

Aquarius monkey This sign is very good for monkeys. It allows their creativity to blossom and Aquarius lends a visionary aspect to their work. They may appear independent, but, at heart, Aquarius monkeys need to be loved and appreciated.

Pisces monkey Pisces is spiritual; the monkey is clever. Together, they create intuitive and impressionable people. Pisces monkeys often appear eccentric, when, in fact, they just have rather unique thought processes.

Some famous people born in the years of the monkey and their zodiac signs

- **René Descartes**
  Philosopher
  31 Mar 1596 Aries

- **John Milton**
  Poet
  9 Dec 1608 Sagittarius

- **Christopher Wren**
  Architect
  20 Oct 1632 Libra

- **Marquis de Sade**
  Writer
  2 Jun 1740 Gemini

- **Lord Byron**
  Poet
  22 Jan 1788 Aquarius

- **Charles Dickens**
  Writer
  7 Feb 1812 Aquarius

- **Paul Gauguin**
  Painter
  7 Jun 1848 Gemini

- **F. Scott Fitzgerald**
  Novelist
  24 Sep 1896 Libra

- **Joan Crawford**
  Actress
  23 Mar 1908 Aries

- **Bette Davis**
  Actress
  5 Apr 1908 Aries

- **James Stewart**
  Actor
  20 May 1908 Taurus

- **Ian Fleming**
  Novelist
  28 May 1908 Gemini

- **Claude Lévi-Strauss**
  Anthropologist
  28 Nov 1908 Sagittarius

- **Walter Matthau**
  Actor
  1 Oct 1920 Libra

- **Elizabeth Taylor**
  Actress
  27 Feb 1932 Pisces

- **John Updike**
  Writer
  18 Mar 1932 Pisces

- **Peter O'Toole**
  Actor
  2 Aug 1932 Leo

- **Diana Ross**
  Singer
  26 Mar 1944 Aries

- **Bjorn Borg**
  Tennis player
  6 Jun 1956 Gemini

- **Sebastian Coe**
  Athlete/Politician
  29 Sep 1956 Libra

10. The Rooster
The Yin metal animal

Lunar years ruled by the rooster			
1909	22 Jan 1900	–	18 Feb 1910
1921	8 Feb 1921	–	27 Jan 1922
1933	26 Jan 1933	–	13 Feb 1934
1945	13 Feb 1945	–	1 Feb 1946
1957	31 Jan 1957	–	17 Feb 1958
1969	17 Feb 1969	–	5 Feb 1970
1981	5 Feb 1981	–	24 Jan 1982
1993	23 Jan 1993	–	9 Feb 1994
2005	9 Feb 2005	–	28 Jan 2006

In China, the rooster is associated with the five virtues: fortune, courage, goodness, confidence and military honour.

THE ROOSTER PERSONALITY

Roosters are flamboyant people. Appearance is very important to them and roosters are constantly improving themselves as they are never satisfied with how they look. Roosters are also friendly, pleasant and obliging people. At times of crisis, they prove themselves to be resourceful and talented. Roosters have the wisdom to take life as it comes and keep their attitudes relaxed. They are genuinely independent and rely on none but themselves for moral support and for solutions to their problems.

CHARACTERISTICS

These are the general personality traits of those people who are typical roosters, both at their best and at their worst.

Positive	Negative
● honest	● vain
● obliging	● thoughtless
● courageous	● self-preoccupied
● flamboyant	● arrogant
● resilient	● vulnerable
● enthusiastic	● critical
● relaxed	● superior
● cultivated	● argumentative
● loyal	● harsh
● sincere	● boastful
● capable	● dissipated
● generous	● ostentatious
● charitable	● pretentious
● entertaining	● embellishes the truth

SECRET ROOSTER

For all their bluff and bravado, in reality roosters are very sensitive and vulnerable people. They are susceptible to both flattery and criticism, and so are easily influenced by either. They hide this weakness behind their arrogant facades. Another little-known fact about roosters is that they like to read. They are actually very knowledgeable people but do not display this aspect of themselves. A rooster would rather be judged on appearance than intelligence.

ELEMENT

Rooster is linked to the ancient Chinese element of metal. This is a very strong element. It can be seen positively as a valuable resource, such as gold; or negatively as a weapon, such as a sword. For example, the energy of metal expresses itself supportively and inspirationally as well as destructively and inflexibly. Metal people are also intuitive and ambitious.

BALANCE

Chinese tradition holds that the lives of roosters will be filled with ups and downs. They will experience both the joys and sorrows that life has to offer; for example, sometimes poor and at other times rich. Roosters should aim to achieve emotional stability. They must balance their larger-than-life images with their vulnerable inner selves. Only then will their lives become calm and productive.

BEST ASSOCIATIONS

Traditionally, the following are said to be associated with roosters:

Taste	pungent
Season	autumn
Birth	spring
Colours	yellow, white
Plant	orange and palm trees
Flower	sunflower
Food	cereals
Climate	dry

 ## THE MALE ROOSTER

If a man has a typical rooster personality, he will generally display the behaviour listed below.

- is charming
- is attracted to difficult situations
- has a tendency to be a braggart
- is brutally frank
- has a good memory
- is jealous of rivals
- appears indifferent
- is a real spendthrift
- may be a dandy
- tells great stories
- is entertaining and witty
- likes the company of women

THE FEMALE ROOSTER

If a woman has a typical rooster personality, she will generally display the behaviour listed below.

- is not malicious
- does not tell white lies
- is reasonable
- is social and communicative
- applies herself totally to whatever she does
- is not as secretive as male roosters
- keeps her promises
- is secretly a jealous person
- appears frivolous
- is good at dealing with catastrophes
- is generous with friends

THE ROOSTER CHILD

If a child has a typical rooster personality, he or she will generally display the behaviour listed below.

- is alert and curious
- responds to reasoning
- has many interests and hobbies
- is rebellious if discouraged
- is easy to live with
- will be a daredevil
- is secretive
- likes being independent
- is good with brothers and sisters
- dislikes solitude
- is well organized

ROOSTER AT HOME

A typical rooster is very adaptable and can feel at home anywhere. If they can, roosters will indulge their extravagant tastes in their homes. Although expensive, furniture is likely to be simple in design. On the whole, roosters will try to create a harmonious and comfortable home. They love gadgets and novelties. Anything that makes life easier or more comfortable, roosters will install in their home. Roosters are obsessive about cleanliness and order in their home, and they keep even little-used cupboards neat and tidy. Ideally, roosters should have a room, 'den' or at least a corner of a room set aside for their sole use. Roosters need a space purely for themselves, where they can gather their wits.

ROOSTER AT WORK

As they are not blessed by good fortune, roosters have to work hard to achieve success. This is not a problem as roosters give their all to their work and are conscientious. Roosters can succeed in any profession that requires nerve, self-confidence and charisma. Therefore, they are suited to anything concerned with selling and also commercial professions. Roosters are too conspicuous to be doing anything discreet and too tactless to be diplomats. They are interested in topical events and dislike routine. Roosters would enjoy working in the media, perhaps on a news-based television show or as a journalist for a newspaper. Roosters are reasonably ambitious and do not like subordinate positions. They are more likely to be head of a department than managing director though, as roosters prefer to avoid undue stress.

Some typical rooster occupations

- newsreader
- sales person
- sales director
- restaurant owner
- hairdresser
- public relations officer
- actor
- farmer
- critic
- manicurist

- teacher
- waiter
- journalist
- travel writer
- beautician
- dentist
- surgeon
- soldier
- fireman
- security guard
- police officer

ROOSTER PREFERENCES

Likes
• seductions
• receiving admiring looks
• serious conversations
• ostentatious displays of wealth
• putting on a show
• tidiness
• occasional periods of solitude
• flattery
• to dream
• to give advice
• spending money
• to make an entrance

Dislikes
• losing their composure
• to be asked direct, personal questions
• badly dressed people
• to display their knowledge
• interference in their affairs
• keeping their opinions to themselves
• to confide in anyone
• practical jokes played on them

GOOD FRIENDS FOR ROOSTERS

The diagram below shows the compatibility of the rooster with other animals. There is no fixed ruling, however, because there are other influences on both the rooster and any potential friend. These influences are:

- the companion in life (see pp. 23–25)
- the dominant element (from the year of birth)

Compatibility of rooster with other animals

■ Rat	■ Dragon	■ Monkey
▲ Ox	▲ Snake	▼ Rooster
○ Tiger	● Horse	○ Dog
▼ Rabbit	○ Goat	● Pig

Key

▲ Highly compatible

● Amicable

■ No conflict but needs some effort

○ Lack of sympathy

▼ Antagonistic

Rat with rooster These two have very little in common. No serious relationship is likely to develop unless there are other strong influences. Competitive rat finds rooster's attention-grabbing behaviour annoying.

Ox with rooster These two are highly compatible. Sociable rooster complements ox's steady nature and ox will allow rooster to show off. They both care for money and financial security.

Tiger with rooster Initially promising, tiger and rooster are unable to have more than a brief friendship. They have much in common, but will quickly fall to misunderstanding and criticizing each other. Not given to reflection, tiger will most likely fail to see the thoughtful nature behind rooster's swaggering facade.

Rabbit with rooster On no account should these two attempt a serious relationship. Rooster's tendency to voice criticisms will send rabbit running; and rooster will find rabbit unsympathetic.

Dragon with rooster The Chinese believe that dragon inspires rooster. Both can be found in the limelight: roosters for reassurance; dragons as it is their natural habitat. This bolsters their egos, but they may misunderstand the other's motives.

Snake with rooster This is the most ideal couple of Chinese astrology. They balance each other like mind and matter. Snake and rooster both flatter and understand one another.

Horse with rooster These two can get on quite well together. Horse will initiate things and rooster can complete them. They are, however, both sensitive to the opinions of others while being tactless themselves. This could create problems and bruise egos.

Goat with rooster These two have very little in common and cannot understand each other. Although roosters will be able to support goats financially, goats will not be able to give roosters the moral support they need in return.

Monkey with rooster Clever monkey and frank rooster can work well together. Yet they will judge each other on appearance alone and both will find the other superficial. If they can learn not to criticize, these two can make a handsome and sociable couple.

Rooster with rooster Chinese legend holds that two roosters under the same roof make life intolerable for everyone else. They either get along very well or dislike each other intensely. Roosters cannot accept their own faults but are quick to point out those of others, so two roosters are guaranteed to argue.

Dog with rooster Idealistic dog and carefree rooster approach life from different angles. Dog will think rooster self-absorbed and unkind. Rooster hates to be judged by others and will be critical of dog's high moral stance.

Pig with rooster Pig and rooster can be very good friends and true, if not exciting, lovers. Pig can recognize rooster's well-hidden sensitivity and kindness, but rooster will be disarmed by understanding pig.

ROOSTER IN LOVE

To a rooster, love is a responsibility and a challenge, not a casual matter. The organized and analytical approach they have towards love makes them prey to disappointment. After all, things rarely happen to plan in a love affair. Roosters are intense and devoted with their loved ones but they have a tendency to be domineering. Preoccupied with their own needs, desires and longings, roosters do not always make the most sympathetic of partners. They expect their partners to know what mood they are in and act accordingly – to know when to be silent or chatty, for example. The rooster's dislike of confidences is an obstacle to real intimacy. Also, the fact that roosters like to sort out their problems by themselves leaves little room for mutual support in a relationship.

ROOSTER AND SEX

Roosters are bold, ostentatious and confident in bed. They are egocentric, however, and a rooster always comesfirst. Roosters are adept at seduction. First, they stun and impress their target with their flamboyance. Then, they make themselves indispensable to that person and finally make sure their partner is satisfied physically. In this way, roosters are usually successful in seducing and keeping lovers. Roosters are not faithful by nature and cannot resist temptation. They justify their infidelities by blaming their lovers – accusing them of neglect, for example. Partners could try making themselves exceptional in some way if they want to keep a rooster interested.

HEALTH

Rooster's element, metal, is associated with the lungs and the large intestine, so roosters should pay particular attention to keeping these organs in working order. Roosters are often afflicted by respiratory problems and should make sure that they keep fit. This will improve both their health and their psychological balance. To maintain a healthy emotional life, roosters should put aside time to just relax and think, preferably on their own.

LEISURE INTERESTS

The favourite pastimes of roosters are socializing and reading. These very different pursuits are typical of the rooster, who is prone to extremes. Roosters have a busy social life as they are agreeable and entertaining guests. Occasionally, they like to get away from it all and visit some quiet, comfortable hideaway. This gives them a chance to replenish their energies and renew their vigour.

THE ROOSTER YEARS AND THEIR ELEMENTS

The rooster is a Yin metal animal. Each of the rooster years, however, is associated with an element which is said to have its own influence. These elements are wood, fire, earth, metal and water. They influence rooster in a regular sequence, which is repeated every 60 years. In the table overleaf, for example, the rooster year 1909 is an earth year. The next rooster earth year is 60 years later in 1969, and the next will be 2029. Rooster's natural element is metal; the influence of this combines with those of the element of the year of birth. The possible effects of the year elements are listed below.

Lunar years ruled by the rooster and their elements			
1909	22 Jan 1909 –	9 Feb 1910	**earth**
1921	8 Feb 1921 –	27 Jan 1922	**metal**
1933	26 Jan 1933 –	13 Feb 1934	**water**
1945	13 Feb 1945 –	1 Feb 1946	**wood**
1957	31 Jan 1957 –	17 Feb 1958	**fire**
1969	17 Feb 1969 –	5 Feb 1970	**earth**
1981	5 Feb 1981 –	24 Jan 1982	**metal**
1993	23 Jan 1993 –	9 Feb 1994	**water**
2005	9 Feb 2005 –	28 Jan 2006	**wood**

Rooster *Metal–Earth* (1909, 1969)
Steadfast earth and ambitious metal combine to make very resourceful and determined people. These people do not shy away from taking on responsibilities and can quickly get to the root of a problem. Earth, however, lessens the rooster's immediate, dramatic appeal. On closer inspection though, the rooster's penchant for finery reveals itself in small touches – discreet but bizarre jewellery, for instance. Earth roosters are not as talkative as other roosters. This does not mean that they are less outspoken, just not as verbose. The few words they do say are guaranteed to be typically blunt.

Rooster *Metal–Metal* (1921, 1981)
Double metal roosters are trouble. They are the most headstrong of all the roosters. Well organized and precise, metal roosters are great sticklers for detail. They have high expectations of themselves and others. These roosters can

be harshly critical of those who fail to live up to their standards. The vitality of roosters can be constrained by the rigidity of double metal. Roosters are not naturally restrained, so metal roosters can, at times, feel confused and ill-at-ease with themselves. On such occasions, they need to seek out solitude to regain their harmony.

Rooster *Metal–Water* (1933, 1993)
Transparent water combines with clear-thinking metal to add clarity to the already considerable intellectual capabilities of the rooster. Water roosters are capable and adaptable people, proficient in many fields. Less authoritarian than others, they gain support by persuasion rather than by intimidation. Water also helps the rooster's innate sensitivity to surface. Roosters born in water years, therefore, are more sympathetic and easy to relate to than other roosters. The metal in their characters, however, stops them being overwhelmed by these sympathies and helps to focus them into worthwhile causes.

Rooster *Metal–Wood* (1945, 2005)
Wood roosters are enthusiastic and progressive people. Wood releases the rooster's dormant creativity and, with their fine imaginations, wood roosters can do well in arts such as poetry and painting. Wood is also, however, an element that is prone to excesses. Roosters are already aggressive, susceptible and over-the-top, and wood can serve to make these qualities more pronounced. On the positive side, both wood and metal are associated with integrity. Wood tempers

the moral rigidity of metal with kindness. Roosters born in wood years are completely trustworthy and are even capable of discretion.

Rooster *Metal–Fire* (1957, 2017)
Fire and metal combine to make strong, dramatic characters. Although eccentric, fire roosters are always convincing people. Rash, audacious and argumentative, they are never inconspicuous. These roosters are high-fliers. Fire roosters are often exceptional: people of action, leaders, heroes or pioneers. Usually with great success, they single-mindedly pursue their goals. Fire enables the rooster to look ahead to the long-term future and not get lost in details on the way. Fire also strengthens the belligerent nature of roosters.

ROOSTER AND THE ZODIAC OF WESTERN ASTROLOGY

To work out your zodiac sign see p. 26–27. General character traits of roosters of the 12 zodiac signs are given below. Bear in mind that the Western zodiac sign modifies the basic rooster nature – especially in the area of personal relationships.

Aries rooster Aries and rooster are similar in many respects, so these roosters have the qualities and defects of typical roosters, but multiplied many times. Above all else, Aries roosters are courageous people who put all their talents into getting what they want out of life.

Taurus rooster Taurus brings stability to these roosters who are less flamboyant. Steady and dependable, they are always willing to help others. Taurus roosters are not as adaptable as other roosters but make up for this by being good planners.

Gemini rooster Mercurial Gemini and extravagant rooster combine to make these people both inconstant and hyperactive. Cultured and knowledgeable, they have a tendency to be intellectual poseurs.

Cancer rooster All roosters are susceptible to the opinions of others and are easily swayed by criticism or flattery. Cancer roosters take this tendency further and are ruled by their emotions. When feeling insecure, they are depressive, vain and egotistical.

Leo rooster Leo roosters are honest, noble, proud, vain and only happy when they are the centre of attention. They are clever at disguising this egotism with acts of generosity, which are actually done to make the rooster feel good rather than the recipient.

Virgo rooster Precise and critical, Virgo roosters are argumentative perfectionists – their comments are usually accurate though. Underneath, Virgo roosters are full of self-doubt and lack confidence.

Libra rooster These roosters are talkative people yet they are not outspoken – they are capable of diplomacy. Libran roosters are proud, indecisive and have a highly developed aesthetic sense.

Scorpio rooster Scorpio roosters have the 'gift of the gab' and are very persuasive people. Combined with their competitive natures, these are not people to get into a verbal sparring match with. They will be high achievers in any profession they choose.

Sagittarius rooster Sagittarius makes these roosters less ostentatious than their fellows. These roosters are still enthusiastic and excitable, of course, but not as pretentious. They have a more holistic approach to life and like to travel.

Capricorn rooster The least boastful of all roosters, Capricornean ones know that a conservative image is more suitable to achieve the material success they crave. They make loyal and devoted lovers but their intellectual lives are fuller than their love lives.

Aquarius rooster More flamboyant and eccentric than any other rooster, Aquarian roosters are unique people. Despite this, they are not arrogant and despise this trait in others. These roosters are broad-minded idealists who are sincere and generous.

Pisces rooster Pisces makes the rooster more sensitive and vulnerable. Pisces roosters are lacking in self-confidence and cannot be relaxed and happy until they have reached a state of financial and domestic security.

Some famous people born in the years of the rooster and their zodiac signs

- **Georg Philipp Telemann**
  Composer
  14 Mar 1681 Pisces

- **David Livingstone**
  Explorer
  19 Mar 1813 Pisces

- **Søren Kierkegaard**
  Philosopher
  5 May 1813 Taurus

- **Richard Wagner**
  Composer
  22 May 1813 Gemini

- **Johann Strauss**
  Composer
  25 Oct 1825 Scorpio

- **August Strindberg**
  Writer
  22 Jan 1849 Aquarius

- **William Faulkner**
  Novelist
  25 Sep 1897 Libra

- **Joseph Goebbels**
  Nazi official
  29 Oct 1897 Scorpio

- **James Mason**
  Actor
  15 May 1909 Taurus

- **Katharine Hepburn**
  Actress
  8 Nov 1909 Scorpio

- **Dirk Bogarde**
  Actor/Writer
  28 Mar 1921 Aries

- **Peter Ustinov**
  Actor/Producer/
  Writer
  16 Apr 1921 Aries

- **Deborah Kerr**
  Actress
  30 Aug 1921 Virgo

- **Michael Caine**
  Actor
  14 Mar 1933 Pisces

- **Philip Roth**
  Writer
  19 Mar 1933 Pisces

- **Joan Collins**
  Actress
  23 May 1933 Gemini

- **Mary Quant**
  Fashion designer
  11 Feb 1934 Aquarius

- **Eric Clapton**
  Musician
  30 Mar 1945 Aries

- **Goldie Hawn**
  Actress
  21 Nov 1945 Scorpio

- **Dolly Parton**
  Singer/Actress
  19 Jan 1946 Capricorn

11. The Dog
The Yang metal animal

Lunar years ruled by the dog					
1910	10 Feb 1910	–	29 Jan	1911
1922	28 Jan 1922	–	15 Feb	1923
1934	14 Feb 1934	–	3 Feb	1935
1946	2 Feb 1946	–	21 Jan	1947
1958	18 Feb 1958	–	7 Feb	1959
1970	6 Feb 1970	–	26 Jan	1971
1982	25 Jan 1982	–	12 Feb	1983
1994	10 Feb 1994	–	30 Jan	1995
2006	29 Jan 2006	–	17 Feb	2007

In China the dog is associated with justice and compassion. Dogs are often described as being the 'champions of the underdogs'.

THE DOG PERSONALITY

Essentially, dogs are honest and noble creatures. They are renowned for being champions of justice and have a tendency to see things in black and white. Dogs are respected for their lively minds and quick tongues, which they use in defence of their chosen cause. Yet dogs are cynics as well as idealists, which produces characters with high moral standards, but they are beset by doubts and anxieties.

CHARACTERISTICS

These are the general personality traits of those people who are typical dogs, both at their best and worst.

Positive	Negative
● loyal	● cynical
● tolerant	● anxious
● idealistic	● pessimistic
● understanding	● suspicious
● dutiful	● timid
● moralistic	● strict
● faithful	● discouraging
● unselfish	● doubtful
● noble	● discontented
● imaginative	● fatalistic
● honest	● obstinate
● courageous	● distrustful
● responsible	● shy
● witty	● introverted
● trustworthy	● unadventurous
● sensitive	● tasteless

Secret dog

Despite their courageousness and determination to do good, dogs need to be led. Left on their own, they can become confused and anxious. After all, there are so many deserving causes and not enough time to help everyone. Once they have been given instructions or help, they can move mountains to carry out a task.

Element

Dog is linked to the ancient Chinese element of metal. This is a very strong element. It can be seen positively as a valuable resource, such as gold; or negatively as a weapon, such as a sword. The energy of metal expresses itself in dogs as their strong-minded, idealistic traits. Metal people are usually ambitious; dogs, however, are not personally ambitious. Instead, they are more concerned with the advancement of the downtrodden.

Balance

The main character fault of dogs is their constant worrying and self-doubting natures. A certain amount of stress or anxiety can be useful as it helps motivate the dog, who lacks motivation. But dogs can worry to the extent that it stops them doing anything useful. This interferes with their ability to lead happy and productive lives. Anxious of the future and regretful of the past, dogs need to learn how to live in the present. If they can take each day as it comes, dogs will find that their anxieties lessen. They need to reach a balance between necessary and useful worrying and self-defeating anxiety.

BEST ASSOCIATIONS

Traditionally, the following are said to be associated with dogs:

Taste	pungent
Season	autumn
Birth	daytime
Colours	black, dark blue
Plants	poppies, water lilies
Flowers	orange blossoms, red poppy
Food	oats
Climate	dry

THE MALE DOG

If a man has a typical dog personality, he will generally display the behaviour listed below.

- will be a protective father
- is loyal and faithful to friends and family
- can be unnecessarily defensive
- makes a good ally
- is slow to make close friends
- is quick to criticize the wrongdoings of others
- has an ironic sense of humour
- is prone to depression
- loves to gossip
- can be stubborn
- rarely shows his true feelings

THE FEMALE DOG

If a woman has a typical dog personality, she will generally display the behaviour listed below.

- has a very black sense of humour
- is more ambitious than male dogs
- is gifted and creative
- is lacking in perseverance
- does not compromise
- is impatient
- is attractive
- likes conversation
- is more sociable than the male
- will be critical of those who do not have her high standards

THE DOG CHILD

If a child has a typical dog personality, he or she will generally display the behaviour listed below.

- is sensitive and affectionate
- needs attentive and understanding parents
- is scared of the dark
- will be stable if parents are protective
- resents younger siblings, at first
- is obliging and devoted
- has difficulty adapting to school
- is well behaved and obedient
- likes fantasy and monster stories

DOG AT HOME

Dogs are not renowned for their sense of taste. They are not materialistic people and would rather not spend all their time and money on perfecting their home. Dogs will decorate and furnish their homes according to personal preference, budget and convenience. They are not ones to be dictated to by fashion, unless they actually like the latest design. This does not mean that the home of dog will be badly decorated and furnished. In fact, the overall effect is often welcoming, pleasant and personal. It may not be the home of an interior designer, but it will have been put together with care and attention to detail.

DOG AT WORK

Dogs are very capable people. The only obstacle to their success is a lack of motivation. They lack the aggression and ambition needed to put their unique skills to work. Dogs can overcome this by choosing a profession that inspires their idealistic natures; something worthwhile and altruistic, for example, to which they can commit themselves. They will then prove themselves to be hard-working, conscientious and honest. Dogs make good managers as they are able to wield authority with tact and will remain accessible to all their staff. They consider collective interests before personal concerns.

Some typical dog occupations

- priest
- missionary
- nun
- trade union leader
- teacher
- charity worker
- nurse
- doctor
- judge
- lawyer
- scientist
- researcher
- critic
- social worker
- legal aid lawyer
- community worker

DOG PREFERENCES

Likes

- anything arcane or concerned with the occult
- horror movies
- natural fabrics
- detective novels
- to remember birthdays
- writing letters to friends
- learning about other cultures
- silver jewellery
- reunions with old friends

Dislikes

- pedants
- hypocrites
- selfish behaviour
- deceit and dishonesty
- family reunions
- smart cocktail parties
- superficial and ambitious people
- psychological game-playing
- man-made fabrics
- counting the financial cost of an activity

GOOD FRIENDS FOR DOGS

The diagram below shows the compatibility of dog with other animals. There is no fixed ruling, however, because there are other influences on both the dog and any potential friend. These influences are:

- the companion in life (see pp. 23–25)
- the dominant element (from the year of birth)

Compatibility of dog with other animals

● Rat	▼ Dragon	● Monkey
○ Ox	■ Snake	○ Rooster
▲ Tiger	▲ Horse	● Dog
● Rabbit	■ Goat	▲ Pig

Key

▲ Highly compatible
● Amicable
■ No conflict but needs some effort
○ Lack of sympathy
▼ Antagonistic

Rat with dog These two live in different worlds. While they can be quite friendly towards each other, their prospects are not good. Dog's passion for fair play will clash with rat's tendency to exploit.

Ox with dog Imaginative dog will not be happy with staid ox. Dog is likely to criticize ox for lacking a sense of humour. If they can learn to respect each other, however, they can get along as both are loyal and faithful.

Tiger with dog The different natures of these two actually complement each other perfectly. Anxious dog will curb tiger's excessive risk-taking; tiger will appreciate dog's loyalty. The relationship could prove long-lasting and stable. Both are idealists, and can combine their talents to achieve great things for a good cause.

Rabbit with dog Loyal dog gets on well with rabbit and the two can have a happy relationship as long as they do not take each other for granted.

Dragon with dog Intellectual but cynical dog will deflate dragon's self-confidence. Dogs are able to see through dragon's image for the mirage it is, so they are unable to admire dragon.

Snake with dog Idealistic dog is attracted to snake's wisdom and depth and can ignore snake's selfish, ambitious streak. Snake will admire dog's honesty and as long as snakes do not mind being idealized, this relationship could work out. It may be, however, that mutual respect will not be matched by a mutual passion.

Horse with dog This is a case of opposites that attract. Horses appreciate dogs' loyal and generous natures and their ability to see things as they really are. In turn, dogs take great pleasure in the company of lively horses and will ignore their waywardness.

Goat with dog Goat and dog can be friends if they apply their tolerant natures to ignoring the other's differences. Normally, however, whimsical goat and dutiful dog just irritate each other.

Monkey with dog This combination can work out well. Dog is attracted by monkey's liveliness and monkey appreciates dog's stability and broad-mindedness. Although there will be a good mutual understanding, both are cynical, and idealistic dog will be suspicious of more realistic monkey's motives.

Rooster with dog Idealistic dog and carefree rooster approach life from different angles. Dog will think rooster self-absorbed and unkind. Rooster hates to be judged by others and will be critical of dog's high moral stance.

Dog with dog Dogs are genuine people and two together can have a warm and understanding, if not exciting, relationship. They will be very dependent on each other and a sharp remark or criticism can easily trigger a major row.

Pig with dog Pleasure-loving pig brings optimism and a carefree aspect to any relationship between these two. This is very beneficial for dog, who will be happy and relaxed with pig. Both are also generous, kind and honest people who, together, can build a lasting relationship.

DOG IN LOVE

Dogs are easy people to love. They are warm, kind and generous. Dogs, however, are not quick to fall in love themselves. They are suspicious and distrustful of people at first. If they meet someone who lives up to their high ideals, dogs will allow themselves to slowly fall in love with that person. Once committed, a dog will want to share everything with their partner and will be affectionate and tender. In return, dogs expect their partners to be everything to them: lover, best friend, confidant, parent and muse. Dogs are not always happy in love as they have such high expectations. Also, they are anxious people who need constant reassuring. Although they are stable characters themselves, their pessimism and anxiety makes it difficult for their partners to feel secure with them.

DOG AND SEX

Although dogs are sensual and passionate people, they value companionship and trust above physical intimacy. A dog cannot live without tenderness and prefers long relationships to brief flings. Nonetheless, dogs are anxious for approval and will try to please their lover. They are faithful by nature and know how to resist temptation. A dog will be destroyed by the infidelity of a lover, yet they can poison a relationship with unfounded suspicions. Compassionate and idealistic, dogs are easily seduced by vulnerable people who need rescuing.

HEALTH

Dog's element, metal, is associated with the lungs and large intestine, so dogs should pay particular attention to keeping these organs in working order. Dogs are anxious people and therefore prone to insomnia and stress-related illnesses. Dogs should try and maintain a balanced approach to life and not become eaten up by worry. Being Yang people, dogs are generally of sound physical health. They should make sure, however, that they watch their weight.

LEISURE INTERESTS

Dogs are sociable and enjoy spending time with friends. They are not particularly adventurous people: a dog is happier going to the cinema or to a good restaurant than rock climbing. They enjoy visiting restaurants that serve foreign cuisine – although it has to be authentic – or just going for a coffee and a chat to the local café. Somewhere peaceful and friendly where they can discuss the wrongs of the world and how to put them right is preferred. For exercise, dogs like simple sports that they can incorporate into their lifestyle easily; swimming in the morning or cycling to work, for example.

THE DOG YEARS AND THEIR ELEMENTS

The dog is a Yang metal animal. Each of the dog years, however, is associated with an element which is said to have its own influence. These elements are wood, fire, earth, metal and water. They influence dog in a regular sequence, which is repeated every 60 years. In the table below, for example, the dog year 1922 is a water year. The next dog water year is 60 years later in 1982, and the next will be 2042. Dog's natural element is metal; the influence of this combines with those of the element of the year of birth. The possible effects of the year elements are listed below.

Lunar years ruled by the dog and their elements			
1910	10 Feb 1910 –	29 Jan 1911	**metal**
1922	28 Jan 1922 –	15 Feb 1923	**water**
1934	14 Feb 1934 –	3 Feb 1935	**wood**
1946	2 Feb 1946 –	21 Feb 1947	**fire**
1958	18 Feb 1958 –	7 Feb 1959	**earth**
1970	6 Feb 1970 –	26 Jan 1971	**metal**
1982	25 Jan 1982 –	12 Feb 1983	**water**
1994	10 Feb 1994 –	30 Jan 1995	**wood**
2006	29 Jan 2006 –	17 Feb 2007	**fire**

Dog *Metal–Metal* (1910, 1970)
Dogs born in metal years are in their natural element. In China, metal dog years are approached warily as they will either be very bad or very good, but never mediocre. In the same way, metal dogs themselves are capable of extreme behaviour. Dogs are already idealistic, and double metal multiplies this tendency twofold. Metal dogs are therefore very principled to the point of being inflexible. This can make metal

dogs towers of strength, but their inability to compromise may be their downfall.

Dog *Metal–Water* (1922, 1982)

Dogs come into their own in this element. Yin water balances with the dog's own innate Yang tendency. Chinese tradition holds that water dogs are the most beautiful and sensual of all the animal signs in the Chinese zodiac. Water erodes the harder edges from dogs, making them charming as well as sexy. Water year-born dogs are more contemplative and intuitive than other dogs. They are less rigid than their natural element, metal, usually dictates and are instead very liberal.

Dog *Metal–Wood* (1934, 1994)

Wood and metal together produce popular and charismatic individuals. Wood allows the dog to appraise situations with more open minds than otherwise. They do not see everything in black and white as most dogs do. They can devote themselves to a cause without becoming obsessional. Wood allows the dog's dormant creativity to blossom. These people are interested in the arts even if they are not creative themselves.

Dog *Metal–Fire* (1946, 2006)

Yang fire enhances the dog's innate Yang tendency. Fire quells their doubts and helps them to be optimists rather than pessimists. Fire dogs are unusually charismatic and flamboyant dogs, but in a friendly and approachable way. These dogs are less egalitarian than other dogs, and are not afraid to put themselves first. Fire dogs are enthusiastic and curious. They should make sure, however, that they control their excessive tendencies and do not become addictive personalities.

Dog *Metal–Earth* (1958, 2018)
Earth dogs are well-balanced people. They are generally happy and stable. Earth gives dogs the ability to take each day as it comes and not to be so anxious about the future. These dogs are, of course, still idealists, but earth imparts efficiency which enables them to put their ideals to some practical use. Earth dogs are materialistic for dogs, but only relative to others of the breed.

 ## DOG AND THE ZODIAC OF WESTERN ASTROLOGY

To work out your zodiac sign see p. 26–27. General character traits of dogs of the 12 zodiac signs are given below. Bear in mind that the Western zodiac sign modifies the basic dog nature – especially in the area of personal relationships.

Aries dog In some ways, Aries helps to balance the dog. Those born under this sign are more relaxed, less serious and more energetic. In other ways, Aries accentuates some of the dog's traits. Arien dogs are incredibly strong-minded and extremely idealistic.

Taurus dog Dogs born under this sign benefit from the sensible and constructive talents of Taurus. These dogs, however, are the most materialistic of all and the males can be chauvinistic.

Gemini dog Intellectual Gemini and ethical dogs are prone to theorizing about the causes of the world's problems. Gemini also increases the dog's already nervous disposition and these people can be unstable.

Cancer dog Cancer dogs often appear cold and indifferent, but underneath they are among the most sensitive and vulnerable of all the animal signs. They are primarily family-orientated people.

Leo dog The most direct and honest of all the dogs, Leo ones despise being manipulated. They are spontaneous and energetic people who are unusually flamboyant, and even egotistical, for dogs.

Virgo dog Critical Virgo adds bite to the dog's nature. These people are kind but not necessarily gentle. This applies to how they perceive themselves as well as others. Virgo dogs can be too critical of themselves and this increases their anxiety.

Libra dog Refined and intelligent, Libran dogs are sociable animals. They are open to compromise as they are not aggressive enough to get their own way.

Scorpio dog Self-righteous and aggressive, Scorpio dogs are not sociable animals. They are nevertheless compassionate people at heart. These dogs find it hard to be faithful as they cannot resist temptation.

Sagittarius dog These dogs are intrigued by different cultures and other viewpoints. Although others may find their broad-mindedness a bit impersonal, they are still passionate about justice.

Capricorn dog Conservative and materially successful, Capricorn dogs are often 'pillars of the community'. They have a strict sense of duty and responsibility and are very moralistic.

Aquarius dog Eccentric Aquarius and constant dog combine to produce highly individualistic people. They each have a uniquely personal outlook on life. All of them have well-developed communication skills.

Pisces dog Pisces dogs are a strange combination of strong minds with weak wills. All dogs are plagued by self-doubt, and Pisces dogs are at times incapacitated by this. They should beware of others taking advantage of this weakness.

Some famous people born in the years of the dog and their zodiac signs

- **François Voltaire**
  Philosopher
  21 Nov 1694 Scorpio

- **Benjamin Franklin**
  Statesman
  17 Jan 1706 Capricorn

- **Victor Hugo**
  Novelist
  26 Feb 1802 Pisces

- **Georges Bizet**
  Composer
  25 Oct 1838 Scorpio

- **Claude Debussy**
  Composer
  22 Aug 1862 Leo

- **Harry Houdini**
  Escapologist
  6 Apr 1874 Aries

- **Winston Churchill**
  Statesman
  30 Nov 1874 Sagittarius

- **Bertolt Brecht**
  Writer
  10 Feb 1898 Aquarius

- **George Gershwin**
  Composer
  26 Sep 1898 Libra

- **René Magritte**
  Artist
  21 Nov 1898 Scorpio

- **Judy Garland**
  Actress
  10 Jun 1922 Gemini

- **Pierre Cardin**
  Fashion designer
  7 Jul 1922 Cancer

- **Yuri Gagarin**
  Astronaut
  9 Mar 1934 Pisces

- **Shirley MacLaine**
  Actress
  24 Apr 1934 Taurus

- **Sophia Loren**
  Actress
  20 Sep 1934 Virgo

- **Elvis Presley**
  Singer
  8 Jan 1935 Capricorn

- **Liza Minnelli**
  Singer/Actress
  12 Mar 1946 Pisces

- **Cher**
  Singer/Actress
  20 May 1946 Taurus

- **Sylvester Stallone**
  Actor
  6 Jul 1946 Cancer

- **Michael Jackson**
  Singer
  29 Aug 1958 Virgo

12. The Pig
The Yin water animal

Lunar years ruled by the pig			
1911	30 Jan 1911	–	17 Feb 1912
1923	16 Feb 1923	–	4 Feb 1924
1935	4 Feb 1935	–	23 Jan 1936
1947	22 Jan 1947	–	9 Feb 1948
1959	8 Feb 1959	–	27 Jan 1960
1971	27 Jan 1971	–	14 Feb 1972
1983	13 Feb 1983	–	1 Feb 1984
1995	31 Jan 1995	–	18 Feb 1996
2007	18 Feb 2007	–	6 Feb 2008

In China, the pig is associated with fertility and virility. To bear children in the year of the pig is considered very fortunate, for they will be happy and honest.

THE PIG PERSONALITY

Pigs are among the most natural and easy-going personalities around. They are pleasure-loving characters who seek out the good and the fun things in life. Pigs are sympathetic and will always be there for friends at times of trouble. In turn, they look to their friends for advice and support when difficult decisions have to be made. Pigs still like to maintain their independence though and privacy is very important to them.

CHARACTERISTICS

These are the general personality traits of those people who are typical pigs, both at their best and at their worst.

Positive	Negative
● eager	● indulgent
● optimistic	● impatient
● fortunate	● excessive
● tolerant	● spendthrift
● careful	● gullible
● sensual	● debauched
● courteous	● fierce-tempered
● uncomplaining	● fearful
● determined	● hesitant
● generous	● materialistic
● peaceful	● naive
● honest	● defenceless
● diligent	
● cheerful	

SECRET PIG

The western view of pigs attributes to them various negative qualities such as greediness, laziness, filthiness and stupidity. In fact, pigs are none of these things – although they do have a taste for good food. They are not overwhelming characters, but they are careful and determined people who are not easily set back by obstacles.

ELEMENT

Pig is linked to the ancient Chinese element of water. Water is linked to the arts and inner expressiveness. Emotionally, water is associated with fear. It also endows sensitivity and understanding. In pigs, water expresses itself as their nurturing qualities and in their ability to compromise and avoid conflict.

BALANCE

The pig is a Yin animal that exemplifies the Yin principles of peace, rest and harmony. On the whole, therefore, pigs are well-balanced people. Their lives will not suffer from the ups and downs typical of the more unbalanced animal signs such as the dragon and the horse. Indeed, the Chinese astrological symbol for the pig is a set of balanced scales.

BEST ASSOCIATIONS

Traditionally, the following are said to be associated with pigs:

Taste	salt
Season	winter
Birth	winter
Colours	black
Plant	ginseng
Flower	water lily
Food	peas, meat
Climate	cold, wet

THE MALE PIG

If a man has a typical pig personality, he will generally display the behaviour listed below.

- is easily deceived
- has impeccable manners
- does not exact revenge on enemies
- is endowed with common sense
- enjoys good food and fine wines
- always sees the best in people
- is a pacifist
- will have a difficult youth

THE FEMALE PIG

If a woman has a typical pig personality, she will generally display the behaviour listed below.

- is famous for her hospitality
- is often taken advantage of
- will always help her friends
- is naturally clever
- is always polite
- will not bear grudges
- is bright and alert
- is eager to learn
- forgives but does not forget

PIG CHILD

If a child has a typical pig personality, he or she will generally display the behaviour listed below.

- is reasonable and peaceful
- daydreams
- is careless
- does not have tantrums
- will sulk if ignored
- needs gentle discipline
- enjoys privacy
- is enthusiastic when happy
- has a sweet tooth
- is even-tempered

PIG AT HOME

Pigs are very sensual as well as domestic people and their homes reflect this. Soft armchairs, deep-pile carpets and huge bathtubs are all favoured by pigs. The home of a pig will not be ostentatious though. They do not decorate to impress – only to please themselves. Pigs like to be able to relax at home. They do not want to be inhibited by thoughts of leaving marks on expensive furniture. All pigs are prone to excesses. At home, they can be either extremely houseproud, tidy people or very slovenly, messy types. One thing is certain, however; the kitchen will be well-stocked and well-equipped. Pigs are gourmets when it comes to food. They love to be creative in the kitchen.

PIG AT WORK

Pigs are not lazy. They are very hard-working and will rarely be unemployed. Although money, status and power are not particularly important to pigs, they do want to achieve a comfortable lifestyle. So, they will do their best to ensure their financial security. Pigs are suited to most kinds of technical, scientific and practical-based work. They are careful and diligent – skills which are ideal for such occupations. Pigs also excel as managers. Attentive and understanding but not weak, they are good at dealing with people. Pigs can take advice, and indeed actually seek it out when faced by a decision. The decisions they make are therefore carefully thought out and never rash.

Some typical pig occupations

- researcher
- scientist
- chemist
- technician
- musician
- restaurateur
- shoemaker
- social worker
- fundraiser
- builder
- chef
- delicatessen owner
- personnel manager
- administrative officer
- gourmet
- Samaritan
- civil servant

PIG PREFERENCES

Likes

- making presents for people
- to be comfortable
- organizing parties
- reading a good book
- famous people
- to gossip
- the sound of applause
- to work as part of a team
- to be in a relationship

Dislikes

- arguments
- making difficult decisions alone
- possessive people
- to be reproached
- talking to people they dislike
- living by their wits alone
- being deceitful
- to feel confused
- to fall out with friends
- inhospitable people
- not knowing where they stand

GOOD FRIENDS FOR PIGS

The diagram below shows the compatibility of pig with other animals. There is no fixed ruling, however, because there are other influences on both the pig and any potential friend. These influences are:

- the companion in life (see pp. 23–25)
- the dominant element (from the year of birth)

Compatibility of pigs with other animals

● Rat	● Dragon	● Monkey
■ Ox	▼ Snake	● Rooster
● Tiger	■ Horse	▲ Dog
▲ Rabbit	▲ Goat	○ Pig

Key

▲ Highly compatible
● Amicable
■ No conflict but needs some effort
○ Lack of sympathy
▼ Antagonistic

Rat with pig This materialistic pair can be very good friends for a while, but trusting pig is rather vulnerable to rat's charms and may end up unable to say no when necessary.

Ox with pig Pig enjoys peace and quiet as much as ox but may find ox's responsible behaviour wearisome at times. Pigs like to go out and enjoy themselves; oxen like to stay at home and relax. Pig may find ox too demanding and ox may find pig irritating.

Tiger with pig These two can get on well together as they are both gregarious, tolerant and independent. Tiger will protect pig from his enemies and pig will prove loyal. Be warned, however, that tiger may be tempted to test pig's temper and find himself at the losing end.

Rabbit with pig Pleasure-loving, tolerant pig is a good match for rabbit. Discreet rabbit may be a bit unnerved by sensual pig's public displays of affection, but this is a minor point.

Dragon with pig Even though pigs and dragons have little in common, the two are actually very compatible. Pigs are easy-going and enjoy dragons' showy nature. Dragon will sweep pig off his feet who, in turn, will adore and fuss over dragon.

Snake with pig This is a case of opposites that do not attract. Snake sees pig as naive and innocent but pig is wise to snake's true nature. Both are very sensual creatures and this can unite them. If a relationship does endure, it is likely to be thanks to pig's forgiving nature. Pigs will not, however, allow themselves to be taken for granted for long.

Horse with pig At first, these two will get along. Pig will find horse exciting and horse will enjoy pig's kind and loving nature. Eventually, however, selfish horse will test pig's patience to the limit, or horse will get bored with the pig.

Goat with pig This is a good alliance for both signs. Both value tranquillity and harmony, and are able to make the concessions necessary to achieve them. Goat should take care not to stretch pig's tolerance too far, however, by acting irresponsibly.

Monkey with pig As both are out-going and friendly, this can be a well-balanced relationship. Monkeys can help generous pigs curb their excessive spending. Honest pig can appreciate the monkey's planning and scheming.

Rooster with pig Pig and the rooster can be very good friends and true, if not exciting, lovers. Pig is one of the few animal signs that can recognize rooster's well-hidden sensitivity and kindness. Rooster will be disarmed by understanding pig.

Dog with pig Contented pig brings optimism and a carefree aspect to pessimistic dog. This is very beneficial for dog, who will be happy and relaxed with pig. Both are also generous, kind and honest people who, together, can build a lasting relationship.

Pig with pig A pig can be a very good friend to another pig. There will be many misunderstandings, however, as they will bring out the worst, selfish side of each other. Also, the relationship may lack enough sparks to keep them both interested for long.

PIG IN LOVE

Pig people are enthusiastic about love. Once they have met someone compatible, they fall in love quickly and deeply. It is obvious to everyone when a pig is in love, as they wear their hearts on their sleeves. Warm-hearted and open people, pigs create peaceful and happy relationships. They will do anything to please the loved one. Pigs are sentimental and may overdo their displays of love and devotion. They should take care not to smother their partners, as not everyone appreciates constant attention. Conversely, pigs also like to maintain an aura of independence, even though at heart they are emotionally dependent on their partners. Pigs are vulnerable when they are in love. If they get hurt badly, then they may become bitter and will not risk the experience again.

PIG AND SEX

Pigs are both amorous and sensual people. They are not shy about sexual matters and know what they like. Even though pigs are romantic, they would rather express their feelings physically than emotionally. If the love of their life does not reciprocate, pigs will quite happily satisfy their desires elsewhere until they can get the person they want. Until they settle down, pigs will have many roller-coaster affairs that end badly – usually for them. But a pig is never depressed for long. Once committed, a pig will be faithful and loyal. To seduce a pig, cook a splendid meal, serve fine wines and let nature take it course.

HEALTH

Pig's element, water, is associated with the kidneys and the bladder, so pigs should pay particular attention to keeping these organs in good working order. Watch out for the symptoms of urinary tract infections and drink plenty of water. Pigs cannot resist good foods, so many have a weight problem. They should try to establish healthy eating patterns and eat less rich foods. For a change, pigs could treat themselves with exotic fruits instead of high fat foods.

LEISURE INTERESTS

Pigs love to read and write. They always keep in touch with old friends, often by letter if they live far away. To relax, pigs like to visit remote and wild landscapes. They can indulge their need for privacy and get involved in some outdoor sports. Rock climbing, abseiling, canoeing and windsurfing all appeal to pigs, who have an adventurous streak. Pigs also enjoy less daring activities such as long country walks. Rambling is ideal for the relaxed and sociable pig. Of course, all pigs enjoy preparing good food. Consulting the latest cookbook, they will try their hand at new and unusual dishes. The preparation is as enjoyable as the consumption for a pig.

THE PIG YEARS AND THEIR ELEMENTS

The pig is a Yin water animal. Each of the pig years, however, is associated with an element which is said to have its own influence. These elements are wood, fire, earth, metal and water. They influence pig in a regular sequence, which is repeated every 60 years. In the table below, for example, the pig year 1911 is a metal year. The next pig metal year is 60 years later in 1971, and the next will be 2031. Pig's natural element is water; the influence of this combines with those of the element of the year of birth. The possible effects of the year elements are listed below.

Lunar years ruled by the pig and their elements		
1911	30 Jan 1911 – 17 Feb 1912	**metal**
1923	16 Feb 1923 – 4 Feb 1924	**water**
1935	4 Feb 1935 – 23 Jan 1936	**wood**
1947	22 Jan 1947 – 9 Feb 1948	**fire**
1959	8 Feb 1959 – 27 Jan 1960	**earth**
1971	27 Jan 1971 – 14 Feb 1972	**metal**
1983	13 Feb 1983 – 1 Feb 1984	**water**
1995	31 Jan 1995 – 18 Feb 1996	**wood**
2007	18 Feb 2007 – 6 Feb 2008	**fire**

Pig *Water–Metal* (1911, 1971)
Normally, the element metal makes a person rigid and pessimistic. The easy-going and optimistic pig, however, relieves these tendencies. Instead, metal pigs are blessed

with immense fortitude and a great deal of perseverance. Metal makes these pigs more ambitious and stubborn than any other. They are extroverts as well as socialites. Unusually for pigs, those born in metal years have sharp wits and incisive intellects. Metal pigs are more brash than other pigs. For these reasons, they are prone to offending people.

Pig *Water–Water* (1923, 1983)
Pigs born in water years are in their natural element. Double water makes these people incredibly diplomatic and highly persuasive. Water pigs are very sympathetic and refuse to hear bad of anybody. They need to learn to be more realistic about others. All pigs are sensual and physically indulgent – water ones doubly so. These people need to find more constructive outlets for this side of their nature. Otherwise, they will become degenerates.

Pig *Water–Wood* (1935, 1995)
Wood and water is a fortunate combination for the pig. Water allows the creative wood element to blossom. These people are communicative and will gather respect and support in whatever field they operate. Consequently, wood pigs often rise to prominent positions. They are wise people who give very good, though not always welcome, advice. Wood pigs should take care not to associate with less scrupulous people who will take advantage of them.

Pig *Water–Fire* (1947, 2007)
Fire increases the excessive tendencies of pig people. Positively aspected, fire pigs are the most brave,

adventurous and optimistic of all pig people, yet the huge energies they have are just as likely to be concentrated on indulging their pleasure-loving natures as plunged into some worthwhile cause. Pigs born in fire years are capable of reaching great heights of achievement or great depths of depravity.

Pig *Water–Earth* (1899, 1959)

Earth steadies the fluid element of water. It is a balancing medium for the pig. Those pigs born in earth years are likely to lead safe, comfortable and secure lives. Most pigs suffer from fear and excessive caution, but earth pigs are not beset by such problems. Consequently, they are more self-confident and assured than pigs usually are. Earth pigs are hard-working and resourceful. They tend to have great physical strength and stamina.

PIG AND THE ZODIAC OF WESTERN ASTROLOGY

To work out your zodiac sign see p. 26–27. General character traits of pigs of the 12 zodiac signs are given below. Bear in mind that the Western zodiac sign modifies the basic pig nature – especially in the area of personal relationships.

Aries pig Impetuous Aries and carefree pig combine to produce youthful, almost child-like people. They are enthusiastic and innocent characters who are well liked by everyone they meet. Aries pigs are also brilliant at both art and management.

Taurus pig Taurus pigs are patient, materialistic and cautious. They can be found in the upper echelons of society among the 'beautiful people'. Pigs born under this sign are not snobs, however; they are generous, kind and understanding to a fault.

Gemini pig Mercurial Gemini does not allow the pig to be as hesitant or indulgent as usual. Gemini pigs are more interested in cerebral matters than physical pleasure. They are outspoken and have a sardonic sense of humour.

Cancer pig Cancer pigs are amazingly self-sufficient. They have self-discipline and great insight. Unfortunately, this assurance can crumble when they feel insecure. Cancer pigs are prone to mood swings and bouts of depression.

Leo pig Leo pigs are larger-than-life characters. They are open, warm-hearted and very generous. A pig born under this sign positively enjoys helping others out. The only bad thing to be said about a Leo pig is that, at times, they are self-centred.

Virgo pig Virgo pigs can appear cold and calculating. They are still typically kind pig people, however, but just a little more discriminating than other pigs. Analytical Virgo makes them less ready with their favours. They will only help those whom they feel really deserve help.

Libra pig Sophisticated Libra lends refinement to the pig. Libran pigs are talented and creative people. Dreamers as well, if they are not careful they will spend all their time with their heads in the clouds.

Scorpio pig Scorpio brings a measure of profundity to the pig. Typically, pigs are credulous people, but not those born under this sign. Scorpio pigs are very suspicious. Pushy and outspoken, these people are driven by the need to secure their financial success.

Sagittarius pig Sagittarius pigs are happy-go-lucky adventurers. They have an enthusiastic and curious approach to life. Although they make loving partners, these pigs cannot stand to feel tied down.

Capricorn pig Capricornean pigs are authoritarian and opportunistic. They want to both succeed materially and impress their contemporaries. Despite this, they are loyal and protective, if a little overpowering, with loved ones.

Aquarius pig Honest and sincere, Aquarian pigs are popular people. They often appear eccentric, however. In fact, these pigs have such a unique perspective on life that they find it difficult to get close to anyone.

Pisces pig Charming, sweet-natured and loving, Pisces pigs are truly nice people. They are renowned for their hospitality but can be unexpectedly mean with their money. Pisces pigs often have healing gifts.

Some famous people born in the years of the pig and their zodiac signs

- **King Henry VIII**
  Monarch
  28 Jun 1491 Cancer

- **Oliver Cromwell**
  Statesman/Soldier
  25 Apr 1599 Taurus

- **Otto von Bismarck**
  Statesman
  1 Apr 1815 Aries

- **Carl Jung**
  Psychologist
  26 Jul 1875 Leo

- **Fred Astaire**
  Dancer
  10 May 1899 Taurus

- **James Cagney**
  Actor
  17 Jul 1899 Cancer

- **Ernest Hemingway**
  Writer
  21 Jul 1899 Cancer

- **Alfred Hitchcock**
  Filmmaker
  13 Aug 1899 Leo

- **Noël Coward**
  Actor/Writer
  16 Dec 1899 Sagittarius

- **Humphrey Bogart**
  Actor
  25 Dec 1899 **Capricorn**

- **Ronald Reagan**
  Actor/US President
  6 Feb 1911 **Aquarius**

- **Tennessee Williams**
  Writer
  26 Mar 1911 **Aries**

- **Ginger Rogers**
  Dancer
  16 Jul 1911 **Cancer**

- **Lucille Ball**
  Actress
  6 Aug 1911 **Leo**

- **Richard Attenborough**
  Filmmaker
  29 Aug 1923 **Virgo**

- **Maria Callas**
  Opera singer
  3 Dec 1923 **Sagittarius**

- **Dudley Moore**
  Comedian/Actor
  19 Apr 1935 Aries

- **Jerry Lee Lewis**
  Musician
  29 Sep 1935 Libra

- **Johnny Mathis**
  Singer
  30 Sep 1935 Libra

- **Elton John**
  Singer
  25 Mar 1947 Taurus